Stand at the
Crossroads

Stand at the
Crossroads

Wisdom From Those
Who Have Been
There and Done That

Fred DePold

Sisters, Oregon

Stand at the Crossroads: Wisdom From Those Who Have Been There and Done That

©2010 by Fred DePold

Scripture quotations marked KJV are taken from the Holy Bible, King James Version. Public Domain. The edition to which I owe much spiritual insight and practical help is the Holy Bible, Newcastle-Upon-Tyne, published by M. Brown in 1787 with "Practical Observations" by Rev. J.F. Ostervald. This beautiful book was given to me as a Christmas present by my sister Renee and her family.

Scripture quotations marked NIV are taken from the Holy Bible New International Version. Copyright © 1973, 1978, 1984, Zondervan.

Scripture Quotations marked CEV are taken from the Contemporary English Bible Version. Copyright © 1995 by American Bible Society.

Scripture quotations marked Message are taken from The Message Bible. Copyright © 1993, 1994, 1995, 1996, 2000, 2001, 2002 by Eugene H. Peterson.

Scripture quotations marked NLT are taken from the New Living Translation Bible. Copyright © 1996, 2004 by Tyndale Charitable Trust. Used by permission of Tyndale House Publishers.

Scripture quotations marked Amplified are taken from the Amplified Bible. Copyright © 1954, 1958, 1962, 1964, 1965, 1987 by The Lockman Foundation.

Submitted for Copyright Case Number 1-133666521

Published by
Deep River Books
Sisters, Oregon
http://www.deepriverbooks.com

ISBN: 1-935265-14-8
ISBN 13: 978-1935265-14-6
Library of Congress Control Number: 2010924147

Printed in the USA

Cover design: Joe Bailen   Interior design: Juanita Dix

Table of Contents

This book is dedicated to everyone

who has struggled with using drugs and

alcohol and desperately wants to quit.

You can do it with God's help.

Never give up.

Acknowledgments

To my wife Lisa, who has stuck it out with me through good times and bad. I love you, Lisa. We have many good times ahead!

I would like to thank Pastor Ken Wilde of Capital Christian Center, Boise, Idaho, for his inspirational teaching and encouragement to keep on going and be the best I can be with God's help. I have included many biblical principles and truths gleaned from his teachings.

To my friend Reverend Charles Ahrens: When I prayed for a mentor, God sent you into my life. You are a true example of how we are to share the gospel with everyone we come into contact with in all areas of life. I miss you.

To my dear mother: Your countless hours of prayer for me when I was going through my issues have had an eternal impact. Thank you.

Introduction

This book talks of life and death, blessings and curses, and the choices each of us make that lead to one or the other. The ancient writings call these decisions "crossroads."

For years, I struggled with addictions that dragged me down wrong paths, until at last I reached a crossroads where I made the decisions necessary to change. What I experienced is very similar to what many Americans face all across the nation today, but they deal with greater pressure than ever before—especially teenagers and young adults.

I challenge you to read this story and take my learning experiences to heart. As you read on, you may think about the pressures you yourself are facing. You may think about areas in which you are being tempted, or areas in which you have caused others to participate in sin. Or maybe you have not been deceived by the king of deception as I was. It is possible that the Holy Spirit will speak to you through this story, and that as a result, you will understand what some of your peers are going through and the temptations they face. If that is the case, I pray that you will be a lighthouse for Jesus, that you will reach out to those around you and share His love. You may be the only Jesus they will ever see.

My intent in writing this story is that the millions of teenagers and young adults struggling or experimenting with drugs and alcohol, the many who think the drug-and-alcohol crowd is "cool," may read this and take to heart the learning experiences of those who have walked the road before them. Together, we will explore the dangers of temptation, look at why you do not have to let your past dictate your future, and realize a way to Reverse the Curse of alcoholism and drug addiction that runs in families, neighborhoods, and social groups.

If after reading this story you think of someone you know who could benefit from reading it—get that person a copy! I am the first to admit that this book will not solve all of your problems or answer all of your questions, but it will point you in a new direction, and if taken seriously, it can help you begin a new life and start living again—just as I did.

Part 1

This Is Your Life

Chapter 1

Let's Party

DO YOU LIKE TO PARTY? What's your drug of choice? Marijuana, pot, dubage, skunk weed, Colombian gold, green weed, weed, joint, hooter, happy weed, beer bong, cocaine, speed, crank, cross tops, black beauties, happy pills, whiskey, party-till-you-puke, or all of the above? I could roll a joint with one hand and was proud of it. Sound fun? Looking back, all I can say was that I was an idiot!

For me, it all started with a friend sneaking a beer out of his dad's refrigerator in the garage. As a result, I spent the next twenty years struggling with alcohol and drugs. I thank God that today I am free from the grips of hell: I am free from drugs and drunkenness once and for all. But it all started with the first drink! Think about it. It took me *twenty years* to break the chains of alcoholism that ran in my family. (Some call these "generational curses.")

When I was a freshman in high school, several of my friends and I were kicked off the football team because we came to

1

practice drunk and stoned. Instead of playing, we would go to the high-school football games and party. On one occasion we had a tequila-drinking contest. I won, but I lost. Sure, I won at chugging tequila, but I passed out and had to be carried in front of the entire stadium. Loser! I thought I was going to die of alcohol poisoning. Mom and Dad were not impressed.

By the age of fifteen I was already a heavy drinker. I managed to go to school and work for my dad, but I could drink all night. My parents were trusting, and I took advantage of it. I would tell them I was going to the movies, that I would drive straight there, watch movies until late, and drive straight home. I don't think I ever did go to the movies—instead my friends and I would fill up the gas tank, buy a case of beer, and head out to party. Generally, one of us had a baggie of weed to go along with the beer. We would drive to the mountains or a local reservoir and party, sometimes with a bonfire and lots of loud rock 'n' roll. The pot progressed to pills, speed, crank, cocaine, and often all of the above.

Dad generally parked his truck in the back of the house. I would push it all the way from the backyard to the front and a little down the street before I started it. Looking back, I don't know how I did it—but the last thing I needed was for him to catch me. Dad was an ex-marine who had worked in law enforcement and the prison system most of his life. He was tough and mean, and he wasn't afraid to use a belt or tree branch for punishment. Nevertheless, I would steal his truck or Mom's station wagon for the night, and we would party all night long. My friends called Mom's station wagon "the welfare wagon."

Many times I would be sick the next day at school. On one occasion, I was a little out of control. We had been drinking tequila and smoking pot. It was two or three in the morning, and a police car turned on its lights right behind me. I pulled over to the wrong side of the street. When they asked me to get out of the truck, I managed to fall out onto the sidewalk. I was arrested and taken to the police station.

When the officer called my dad, I could hear them arguing on the phone. The officer told Dad that I was in custody and that his truck was parked on the side of the road. Dad didn't believe him and said, "No, you must be mistaken, my son is in bed, and my truck is in my backyard." The officer finally convinced Dad to go look, and he came right down to get me. Luckily for Dad, they did not yet have rules about spanking your kids, because he let me have it on the front steps of the police station. Looking back, I don't blame him at all.

You would think that I had learned my lesson, but no, I was just getting started.

While I was in the holding cell at the police station, I noticed that several people had written their names on the wall, the door, and even the ceiling. Several of my new friends had been to this very same holding cell. They were people I thought were cool.

My first car was a Dodge Charger, one of the muscle cars. It ran real well and was as solid as a tank. We often would declare a "Lake Day" at our school. This meant that we would buy a keg of beer, and several of us would ditch school and go to the lake for the day and drink beer. We would charge $2 per person and stamp the hand of everyone who paid. Since most high schoolers didn't drink like we did, they would pay two bucks and have a couple of beers, and we would end up with a free keg of beer.

On one particular occasion, we were rained out. Rather than sit at the lake and get rained on, we loaded the keg into the trunk of my car, routed the hose into the backseat, and took off to the mountains. We ended up crashing through a locked gate and flying over the edge of the road into a pile of rocks. We finally got the car out and took off again, only to discover that we had busted a hole in the oil pan and the engine was fried. This was a typical adventure for us. I honestly believe that God commanded His angels to protect us, because we had so many close calls!

When I was sixteen, I came home one day just sloppy drunk. Dad got all over my case. He said, "I don't mind if you drink a little, but have some common sense. Don't be getting this drunk, and especially don't be driving home." Well, this caused a big fight. I thought he was a jerk and just kept doing my own thing. My parents took off for the coast for a few days, so my friend and I took the opportunity to harvest our pot crop. We hung several plants in the garage to dry. Mom and Dad came home early, only to discover my crop hanging in the garage. They were not impressed.

Shortly thereafter, I was working at a gas station, and my neighbor came up to me and asked, "How much do you want for your weight set?" I told him it wasn't for sale. He then asked how much I wanted for my backpack. I said, "What are you talking about? My stuff is not for sale!" He said, "Aren't you having a garage sale? All your stuff is out in your front yard." Apparently Dad was tired of my crap, and he had thrown all my stuff out of the house. I backed my truck up, loaded it, and lived in my truck for a few days.

My friends soon got tired of me bumming off them. My sister helped me get into my own apartment, but as you can imagine, it became the party pad. I now had no one to answer to. I partied every day after work until I passed out.

People told me that pot and alcohol would lead to other drugs. They said they knew this from experience. I told them they were wrong—that wouldn't happen to me. They were right! Cocaine, speed (we called it crank), mushrooms, pills—partying became a mixture of many things. I could go on and on, but I think you are starting to get the picture. Those of you who can relate to this lifestyle already know the scene. You know all about this way of life, its ups and downs. Hangovers, alcohol poisoning, not knowing what happened the night before. Hearing from friends that you did or said something you are now ashamed of.

Even though I was such a drunk, I managed to hold down a job. I was told I was a functional alcoholic. Just what is that? It is someone who gets through life but is drunk most of the time. Let me describe it for you. I went to work no matter what, and I paid my bills even though I was sick at work many times. I remember getting ready for work one morning. I was still drunk from the night before. I showered, shaved, brushed my teeth, and put on my spray deodorant. The problem was, the spray deodorant wasn't deodorant at all—it was hairspray. Well, because I was late and still a little drunk from the night before, I went to work with sticky armpits. This is an example of a functional alcoholic. You get through life, but you do a poor job of it.

Hairspray in the armpits is a funny example, but that "poor job" applies to all areas of life. As a father, a husband, a friend, a son, a brother, and an employee, my so-called party lifestyle robbed me of being all I could be. You might think you are having fun, but believe me, it will catch up to you. When and if you ever make it out of this lifestyle, you will look back on it and feel the same way I do. Many people never make it out; they live an entire life of hurt and devastation that affects family and friends as well. Think about it for a moment; don't just take my word for it. I'll bet you can think of at least one person who has destroyed his or her life through drugs and alcohol. Do you want to end up like that? If you are one who lives this life, please answer this question in your own mind: has your drug or alcohol usage caused you problems, pain, and suffering, or has it given you blessings, prosperity, and happiness?

How can I get it through to you? *Drugs and alcohol can ruin your life!*

Eventually, I discovered the choices I was making were not only affecting me, but those around me: my wife, my parents, my friends, even my children. I only wish I had discovered what a terrible influence I was having at an earlier time in my life. And I do hope you will discover this a lot sooner than I did. Think about it! Do you want to have a positive or negative impact on those in your life? Please read on, and see what happened to me and some of my friends and the impact our decisions had on our friends and families.

Important Points

1. For me, it all started with the first drink. Avoid it like it will kill you!
2. The party crowd you think is cool as a teenager or young adult will often turn out to be the exact opposite later in life.
3. People told me that pot and alcohol would lead to other drugs—they were right, even though I didn't believe it.
4. There is really no such thing as a functional addict. You may get through life and stay out of jail, but you are not being all you can be. I robbed my family of all I could be for them.
5. Simply put: drugs and alcohol can ruin your life.

Chapter 2

Turning Points

AS A FRESHMAN IN HIGH SCHOOL, I became a dealer so I could get my stuff for free. I went from being an honor-roll student in junior high to failing almost every class as a freshman in high school except for phys ed, and that was because the coach smoked pot with us. My eighth-grade football team was district champion, and we were predicted to be state champions our freshman year. But something happened to us. We were introduced to partying—drugs. I was kicked off the football team, along with several classmates. Our team went from district champions to last place the following year.

Don't tell me it's OK to have just one drink or smoke just one joint. I have been there and done that, and it took me twenty years to put it completely behind me. Partying isn't what it's cracked up to be! Yes, it seemed fun at first, but do you think puking your guts out is fun? It's called alcohol poisoning! Do you think waking up in your own puke is fun? Not knowing how you got to where you are? Do you think totaling your seven-day-old, four-wheel-drive truck is fun? How about waking up with a hangover day after day after day—sound fun? How about being curled up in a corner with the feeling that your heart is literally going to explode because you did too much speed? It's a terrible sensation; you can feel every heartbeat. The clock is ticking in slow motion, and you feel like you're going to die.

I tried to stop drinking for a long time. As I've mentioned, I drank for over twenty years. I thought I was never going to quit. I cried out to God on several occasions to forgive me, but I would do it again and again. I could go for a week, sometimes for a couple of weeks, and then I would drink again.

I never did it myself, but I saw my friend shoot up speed. To hear about it or see it on TV is one thing, but to see it in person is quite different. He stuck the needle in his arm, and his eyes rolled back into his head; I could see the instant effect it had on him. It was scary, and I said, "I'm out of here!" The last I heard, he was on the run, wanted for his crimes. He started by sneaking a beer here or there. Then came the offer of the first hit off a joint. That soon led to other drugs and a lifetime of misery.

I remember arguing that marijuana does not lead to other drugs, but I was wrong. It not only happened to me, but to many of my friends. If you have not been tempted, thank God. When and if you ever find yourself in that situation, look beyond the joint, drink, or whatever else you're offered. Look beyond the person offering it, and see what is behind it: your enemy, that ancient serpent spoken of in Genesis 3, the king of deception. He just wants to destroy you, for the Bible says that he seeks to kill, steal, and destroy (John 10:10). The Bible says in 1 Peter 5:8, "Be self-controlled and alert. Your enemy the devil prowls around like a roaring lion looking for someone to devour" (NIV).

Turning Points

Genesis 3 tells the story of when Satan deceived Adam and Eve by telling them that if they ate of the Tree of the Knowledge of Good and Evil, fruit that God had forbidden them to eat, they would become like gods themselves. After hearing this, they looked upon the fruit of the tree and desired it. Then they ate of it, and instantly they felt shamed. We call this true story "the Fall of Man," and they were cast out of the perfect Garden of Eden because of it. So it is with your first joint and your first drink. At first it will look fun: partying with what you think is a cool crowd. Maybe you think you won't "eat of the fruit." But if you hang around them and listen to the deceptive talk about how fun it is, you will start to desire it. Once you partake, you may never overcome without God's help.

Satan is waving bait in front of you. Remember, his goal is to destroy you, and he will try anything. So when you find yourself in a situation where someone is offering you drugs or alcohol, look beyond the person and what he or she is offering. Picture Satan or one of his evil demons standing there offering it to you. But look closer—what do you see? A sharp hook—the drugs and alcohol are just bait on a sharp hook.

I call these encounters with the bait of temptation "Turning Points." Why? Because they can change the direction your life is going.

> *A Turning Point is anything in your life that causes you to change course, either in a positive or a negative direction.*

Either toward Him—that is, our Lord and Savior Jesus Christ, and blessings with Him—or away from Him and toward curses.

You will be faced with many Turning Points in your life. The Bible calls them "crossroads." Jeremiah 6:16 proclaims, "This is what the Lord says: Stand at the crossroads and look; ask for the ancient paths, ask where the good way is, and walk in it, and you will find rest for your souls" (NIV).

The young prophet Jeremiah was sent by the Lord God Almighty to declare this message because the people of Israel had made bad choices. They were living in deep, immoral sin, not a whole lot different from the sin of our day and age.

Jeremiah tells us to stand at the crossroads of our lives, those places where you decide what direction your life will go, and learn from those who have gone before you. In essence, these people have been there and done that: listen to them, learn from them, and you will find peace.

You make these decisions on a regular basis. Jeremiah told Israel to ask for the ancient paths, the tried and true ways of their godly ancestors. He said they should walk in them, and "you will find rest for your souls"! The choice is yours. What do you want out of your life? Destructive habits and devastating addictions—or a life of fulfillment and true success with God's help? Yes, you really can *choose* which way you want your life to go. Good and bad things in life are the result of how you choose to live.

Spiritual Surgery

Once you have the hook of Satan in you, it is difficult to break loose. Some never do, and they live a life of curses or die young. So what if you have already taken a Turning Point in the wrong direction?

Jesus said in Mark 9:42–48 that if your hand causes you to sin, get rid of it, because it is better for you to enter heaven without it than to go to hell with both hands. This is hyperbole—an exaggerated wordplay used to make a point. What Jesus is saying here is that if you have sin in your life, take radical steps to get rid of it.

Sin is like cancer that will grow and can destroy you. What is your cancer? Drugs? Alcohol? Pornography? Gambling? Sexual sin? Witchcraft? Satanism? Only you and God know the answer. You need radical spiritual surgery—get rid of it. Separate yourself from it. You know what sin is in your life; take action now! If not now, when?

Today is a Turning Point in your life. Keep reading. Learn more about the blessings and curses before you. Take the Thirty-Day Challenge outlined in chapters 7 and 8. I dare you! It might help you to talk to a Christian friend or pastor and tell them what you are doing. Ask them to check on you at least once a week during the Thirty-Day Challenge to encourage you to stay on track. Sometimes it helps to have accountability.

It is the choice of a lifetime!

> See, I set before you today life and prosperity, death and destruction. For I command you today to love the Lord your God, to walk in his ways, and to keep his commands, decrees and laws; then you will live and increase, and the Lord your God will bless you in the land you are entering to possess. But if your heart turns away and you are not obedient, and if you are drawn away to bow down to other gods and worship them, I declare to you this day that you will certainly be destroyed. (Deuteronomy 30:15–18, NIV)

Important Points

1. Don't believe that it is OK to have just one drink or smoke just one joint. I have been there and done that. I struggled with it for twenty years before I was able to put it completely behind me.

2. The next time someone offers you drugs or alcohol, look beyond the person and what he is offering. Picture Satan or

one of his demons standing there offering it to you. Picture the drugs or alcohol as bait on a sharp hook. Once the hook is in you, it is difficult to break loose. Some never do, and they live a life of curses or die young.

3. If you have sin in your life, take radical steps to get rid of it. It is like cancer that can grow and destroy you.

4. Be aware of life-defining moments—Turning Points. They can change the direction your life is going; the Bible calls them "crossroads."

5. The Bible tells us to glean from the wisdom of those who have been there and done that. Don't make the same mistakes. Listen and learn from their experiences. They had to learn it the hard way, but you don't have to. The choice is yours.

6. You really can choose which way your life goes.

Chapter 3

Blessings or Curses

DO YOU STILL WANT TO PARTY? Let me tell you about some of the friends I made in junior high and high school, my "party buddies," and how they turned out. I have changed their names, but their situations are real.

Todd married one of the prettiest girls in school. He was like a miniature Hulk. He was the arm-wrestling champion of all. I think he was just born that way. He liked to party, and he did so for many years. Beer and speed were his game. Todd died when he walked the tracks into a speeding train, leaving his wife and three children.

My neighbor Lee shot himself in the head while sitting on a bar stool not far from my house. He was under the influence of God-only-knows-what.

Troy walks the streets and is homeless. He is the skinny man with the wild hair and the eyes that make him look like he is demon possessed. I think he is! If you make eye contact with him, it will make the hair on the back of your neck stand up. I partied often with Troy. He was also into what I called "evil music"—you know, the kind that sounds like demons are singing it.

Another friend, Jeff, has been on hard drugs ever since high school, and I think he shoots up crack now. He was a champion golfer who some said could have gone pro. He was a natural. He has several children, all of whom he is unable to provide for because of his addiction. Last I heard, he was addicted to shooting up speed.

Brad has been in prison for around twenty-five years because he shot and killed a man while trying to rob him in his own home.

Tommy is confined to a wheelchair because he was injured when he crashed his car while under the influence of alcohol, pot, and probably a couple more drugs.

> *Fun, isn't it? Do you still want to party?*
> *Drugs and alcohol can ruin your life!*

Rick, my good friend Rick, was drunk and speeding around the county fairgrounds when he ran into a carload of young girls. I think he killed one and crippled another. Rick's father was also an alcoholic and committed suicide by getting drunk and then sticking a hose in his exhaust pipe and running it into the cab of his truck with the windows rolled up.

Paul's dream was to move to Hawaii and become a big-time drug dealer. Well, he did move to Hawaii and pursue his dream, which ended in the murder of his brother. Someone broke into his brother's apartment, robbed him, and murdered him!

These guys were my friends. They all had one thing in common. They liked to party, and it all started with a sip of beer and their first hit off a joint and then went on to stronger drugs. Listen closely. When you find yourself faced with the decision to party or not, think about my friends. That decision to drink alcohol or smoke pot for the first time can lead you to the same destruction. Don't be deceived by the evil temptations of the world.

The choice is yours! *It is the choice of a lifetime!*

Remember the concept of Turning Points? The decision to party (especially for the first time) can lead to a lifetime of problems and leave a trail of destruction not only for you but also for your family and friends. Think about Todd, Lee, Troy, Jeff, Brad, Tommy, Rick, Paul—my friends. Real people like you. That decision, that choice of a lifetime, can lead you to blessings or to curses.

Deuteronomy 11:26–28 says, "See, I am setting before you today a blessing and a curse—the blessing if you obey the commands of the LORD your God that I am giving you today; the curse if you disobey the commands of the LORD your God and turn from the way that I command you today" (NIV). I believe the principles of the Bible are applicable to our lives today. Don't be deceived by the evil desires of this world. This is your Turning Point. Go for the blessings.

Choose your friends wisely, and don't tell me that it's OK to have just one drink or smoke just one joint. You just heard where it led some of my old party buddies. When you find yourself in that situation, visualize the devil himself offering it to you, because he is the one behind it. Your enemy the devil desires to destroy you.

I first started to write this book about fifteen years ago. I know that times have changed, and there are designer drugs like ecstasy and others, but let me tell you the effect is the same as it's always been. I'm not talking about the high you get from the drug, but about the broken life that results from the party lifestyle. Just three nights ago, my daughter's friends were in a high-speed wreck on the interstate that sent six people to the hospital. They were all partying, and they decided to give someone a ride home at 3 a.m. They were driving over one hundred miles per hour when they ran into the back of a minivan, flipping it upside down and sending them all to the hospital with severe injuries. Now the result of their actions is that some innocent victims may be injured for life.

The driver of the car was drunk and charged with aggravated drunk driving. She is newly married and is now facing a prison sentence. Sound fun? This lifestyle only ends in disaster. Looking at this situation from the outside, one might conclude that it was enough to turn this girl from alcohol abuse, but that doesn't seem to be case. I'm told she's still drinking.

Turning Points change the direction your life is going. Remember, a Turning Point is anything in your life that causes you to change course, either in a positive or a negative direction. You stand at a crossroads, and it's up to you whether you go toward blessings or curses. It's your choice, just like Deuteronomy says.

If you are like I was, a stubborn, rebellious teenager who just wants to have fun, you may not listen. Certain adults warned me not to hang out with the crowd that I did, saying they would only get me in trouble. They were right. I only wish they had broken it down like I'm trying to do for you now. Maybe then I would have listened.

I have many, many more stories. Some of the stupid things my friends and I did would blow you away, but I am too humiliated to put them in writing. I only share these things with you to try to get you to understand the lifestyle my friends and I were living. I am no better than any of them. I just want you to understand what this lifestyle can and often does lead to. As you read on, I am confident you will understand.

Before I end this chapter, here are some statistics you may want to think about.

Marin Institute[1]

- Alcohol is a leading cause of death among youth, particularly teenagers. It contributes substantially to adolescent motor vehicle crashes, other traumatic injuries, suicide, date rape, and family and school problems.
- Every day, on average, 11,318 American youth (twelve to twenty years of age) try alcohol for the first time, compared with 6,488 for marijuana, 2,786 for cocaine, and 386 for heroin.
- Alcohol is by far the most used and abused drug among America's teenagers. According to a national survey, nearly one third (31.5%) of all high-school students reported hazardous drinking (five+ drinks in one setting) during the thirty days preceding the survey.
- Children who are drinking alcohol by seventh grade are more likely to report academic problems, substance use, and delinquent behavior in both middle school and high school. By young adulthood, early alcohol use was associated with employment problems, other substance abuse, and criminal and other violent behavior.
- Young people who begin drinking before age fifteen are four times more likely to develop alcoholism than those who begin drinking at twenty-one.
- More than 1,700 college students in the U.S. are killed each year—about 4.65 a day—as a result of alcohol-related injuries.

National Institute of Alcohol Abuse and Alcoholism[2]

Each year, approximately five thousand young people under the age of twenty-one die as a result of underage drinking; this

---

1. http://www.marininstitute.org/alcohol_policy/violence.htm
2. http://www.niaaa.nih.gov/

includes about 1,900 deaths from motor vehicle crashes, 1,600 as a result of homicides, and 300 from suicide, as well as hundreds from other injuries such as falls, burns, and drownings.

US Bureau of Justice Statistics[3]

On June 30, 2008, 2,310,984 prisoners were held in federal or state prisons or in local jails.

Reported drug and alcohol use by high school seniors, 2007 Used within the last:

Drugs	12 months	30 days
Alcohol	66.4%	44.4%
Marijuana	31.7	18.8
Other Opiates	9.2	3.8
Stimulates	7.5	3.7
Sedatives	6.2	2.7
Tranquilizers	6.2	2.6
Cocaine	5.2	2.0
Hallucinogens	5.4	1.7
Inhalants	3.7	1.2
Steroids	1.4	1.0
Heroin	0.9	0.4

According to the State of Idaho[4], one out of every four Idaho teenagers has at least one sexually transmitted disease. I've heard that the statistic is similar across America.

Are You at Risk?

How do you know if you are at risk? Take this short quiz:

3. http://www.ojp.usdoj.gov/bjs/prisons.htm, http://www.ojp.usdoj.gov/bjs/drugs.htm
4. www.nakedtruth.idaho.gov

Has your partying caused you any harm? Physically, emotionally or financially?

___Yes ___No

Has your partying caused any harm to others?

___Yes ___No

Do you struggle to quit using drugs and/or alcohol?

___Yes___ No

Do you think your life is headed for trouble?

___Yes___ No

If you answered yes to any of the questions above, you may be at risk and in need of help. As you read on, you will learn how you can overcome these issues in your life, turning away from curses toward blessings.

I will tell you how I did it and what worked for me.

Important Points
1. Drugs and alcohol can ruin your life! Hanging out with the wrong crowd can take you down.
2. You stand at a crossroads, and it's up to you whether you go toward blessings or curses.

Chapter 4

The Bible on Blessings or Curses

The Bible is the greatest signpost we have pointing the way to blessings. It shows us the way to God and can help us overcome the strongest temptations in life. We'll talk more about this when we come to the Thirty-Day Challenge. For now, listen to what the Bible says about blessings and curses.

Curses for Disobedience

The written Word of the Lord God Almighty clearly spelled out curses for disobedience for the Israelite people in the days of old. You will find all this in the book of Deuteronomy, chapter 28, starting in verse 15. Read carefully as you hear what the Lord spoke through Moses to the people of Israel.

However, if you do *not* obey the Lord your God and do not carefully follow all his commands and decrees I am giving you today, all these curses will come upon you and overtake you: You will be cursed in the city and cursed in the country. Your basket and your kneading trough will be cursed. The fruit of your womb will be cursed, and the crops of your land, and the calves of your herds and the lambs of your flocks. You will be cursed when you come in and cursed when you go out.

The Lord will send on you curses, confusion and rebuke in everything you put your hand to, until you are destroyed and come to sudden ruin because of the evil you have done in forsaking him. The Lord will plague you with diseases . . . The Lord will strike you with wasting disease, with fever and inflammation, with scorching heat and drought, with blight and mildew, which will plague you until you perish. The sky overhead will be bronze, the ground beneath you iron. The Lord will turn the rain of your country into dust and powder; it will come down from the skies until you are destroyed.

The Lord will cause you to be defeated before your enemies. You will come at them from one direction but flee from them in seven, and you will become a thing of horror to all the kingdoms of the earth. Your carcasses will be food for all the birds of the air and the beasts of the earth, and there will be no one to frighten them away . . . The Lord will afflict you with madness, blindness and confusion of mind. At midday you will grope about like a blind man in the dark. You will be unsuccessful in everything you do; day after day you will be oppressed and robbed, with no one to rescue you. (NIV)

Do you get the point? I am not convinced that you do.

> *Clearly, God will not bless you if you live a life of evil such as the lifestyle drugs and alcohol lead to.*

A close relative of ours was married at a young age. She and her husband were partyers and drug dealers. Nevertheless, they seemed to have everything life had to offer: their own house, jet skis, motorcycles, a race car, several other cars, and two beautiful children. Most of the time they did not work, and they lived well off their income from selling pot and crank.

Today, their lives are a disaster, and their poor children have inherited the curse. The disaster includes a burnt-down apartment with their life's possessions in it and now homelessness. Yet even now, they refuse to turn to the only source that can begin the restoration of their lives. That's right, Jesus. There is no other way. He alone is the way, the truth, and the life. We will talk more about that later.

1. Blessings for Obedience

The written Word of the Lord God Almighty also clearly spelled out blessings for obedience for the Israelite people. You will find them in the book of Deuteronomy, chapter 28, starting in verse 1. Read carefully as you hear what the Lord spoke through Moses to the people of Israel.

> If you fully obey the Lord your God and carefully follow all his commands I give you today, the Lord your God will set you high above all the nations on earth. All these blessings will come

upon you and accompany you if you obey the Lord your God:

You will be blessed in the city and blessed in the country. The fruit of your womb will be blessed, and the crops of your land and the young of your livestock . . . Your basket and your kneading trough will be blessed. You will be blessed when you go in and blessed when you go out. The Lord will grant that the enemies who rise up against you will be defeated before you. They will come at you from one direction but flee from you in seven. The Lord will send a blessing on your barns and on everything you put your hand to. The Lord your God will bless you in the land he is giving you.

The Lord will establish you as his holy people, as he promised you on oath, if you keep the commands of the Lord your God and walk in his ways. Then all the people on earth will see that you are called by the name of the Lord, and they will fear you. The Lord will grant you with abundant prosperity . . . The Lord will open the heavens, the storehouse of his bounty, to send rain on your land in season and to bless all the work of your hands. You will lend to many nations but borrow from none. The Lord will make you the head, not the tail.

If you pay attention to the commands of the Lord your God that I give you this day and carefully follow them, you will always be at the top, never at the bottom. Do not turn aside from any of the commands I give you today, to the right or to the left, following other gods and serving them. (NIV)

The Commandments of God

Obviously, we will be blessed if we follow God's commands. Don't know what they are or how to follow them? Here are the Ten Commandments given to Israel by the Lord God Almighty. The originals are found in Exodus 20:3–17.

1. You shall have no other gods before me.
2. You shall not make for yourself an idol in the form of anything in heaven above or on the earth beneath or in the waters below.
3. You shall not misuse the name of the Lord your God, for the Lord will not hold anyone guiltless who misuses his name.
4. Observe the Sabbath day by keeping it holy.
5. Honor your father and mother.
6. You shall not murder.
7. You shall not commit adultery.
8. You shall not steal.
9. You shall not lie.
10. You shall not covet.

Can You Begin Again?

The Bible is quite clear on this point of blessings or curses. Jesus said in Matthew 7:13–14, "Enter through the narrow gate. For wide is the gate and broad is the road that leads to destruction, and many enter through it. But small is the gate and narrow the road that leads to life, and only a few find it" (NIV).

Let me paraphrase: Life's gateway that leads to death, destruction, and generational curses and ends with an eternity in hell is the easy path, and many take it. But life's gateway leading to blessings and eternal life in the paradise of God is narrow, and few find it.

The choice is yours.

> *You stand at the crossroads — which direction will you go?*

This day I call heaven and earth as witnesses against you that I have set before you *life and death, blessings and curses. Now choose life,* so that you and your children may live and that you may love the Lord your God, listen to his voice, and hold fast to him. (Deuteronomy 30:19–20, NIV, my emphasis.)

This is the choice of a lifetime.
It is not too difficult or beyond your reach.

Now what I am commanding you today is not too difficult for you or beyond your reach. It is not up in heaven, so that you will have to ask, "Who will ascend into heaven to get it and proclaim it to us so we may obey it?" Nor is it beyond the sea, so that you have to ask, "Who will cross the sea to get it and proclaim it to us so we may obey it?" No, the word is very near you; it is in your mouth and in your heart so you may obey it. (Deuteronomy 30:11–14, NIV)

If you have already messed up and broken God's commands, you might be thinking it's too late for you. It isn't. The first thing you must understand is that God forgives you no matter what. The Bible does give commands to follow, but when you repent and ask God for forgiveness, and turn from the lifestyle of sin, He will forgive you! He is a loving God, full of compassion and mercy, slow to anger, abounding in love, forgiving wickedness, rebellion, and sin for those who call upon Him (see Exodus 34:6–7).

Important Points
1. Clearly, God will not bless you if you live a life of evil such as the lifestyles drugs and alcohol lead to.

2. There are natural consequences in life. We reap what we sow—good or bad.
3. God forgives you no matter what.
4. You can turn toward blessings; it is not too difficult or beyond your reach.

Let's Reflect

What is a Turning Point? _____

_____

_____

_____

Drugs and alcohol can ruin your life and have a negative impact on those around you, such as your family, friends, and coworkers. If you have destructive habits, especially drug and alcohol usage, what negative effects have you had on those around you?

_____

_____

_____

_____

Why do you use drugs and alcohol? We all have a reason. Mine was just fun that turned into an addiction—what is yours? Divorce, loss of a loved one, broken family? Write down why you do what you do.

_____

_____

_____

_____

_____

What problems have your addictions and destructive habits caused you?

_____

_____

_____

_____

_____

Are you ready for a change? Do you really want it? Write down the things you want to change in your life.

_____

_____

_____

_____

_____

If you answered honestly, you may be hurting right now because of your answers. But if you do not change, the effect you have on others may potentially get worse. Keep reading: you're about to learn what to do next.

Chapter 5

What Do I Do Now?

IT IS NATURAL TO ASK THIS QUESTION, so let's explore the possibilities.

First of all, think about the direction your life is going. Let's say you are traveling down life's highway. There are many signs ahead. Some of them are warning signs, such as "Danger Ahead," "Beware of Ice on Roadway," "Falling Rock," "25 MPH Curve," "Bridge Out," or, as I found once on an Idaho back road, "Road Gone." It had been washed away in a flood! There are many other signs out there, all of which are there for your guidance and protection and safety for others.

There are many destination signs as well, telling us that if we stay on this road it will lead to a particular destination and how many miles away it is. If you stay on the road your life is on, where will you end up? If there were road signs in

29

your life telling you where you are headed, what would they say? "Life of alcoholism or drugs straight ahead"? "Prison is just a little farther, so stay on course"? "Broken, hurting families ahead"? "Sickness, disease, and poverty"?

There is one sign that you see every so often, but you may just ignore it: this is the sign that says, "Is your life going the wrong direction? God allows U-TURNs."

Do you know what you want out of life? If you feel like your life is headed toward curses—in one of the directions mentioned above—you can make a course correction. Please hear me.

> *You have to line up your direction with*
> *your desired destination.*

You have to purpose to get where you want to be in life.

You can do this. I believe in you. No matter where you are right now, you're standing at a crossroads. You can change. I believe that some of you are going to rise up out of the life-style you are in and become great people. Some of you will raise children who will be world-changers. (If you're a woman with a dream to be a stay-at-home wife and mother who loves, nurtures, supports, and cares for your family through a relationship with Jesus Christ our Lord and Savior, I salute you. I believe there is no greater task a woman can hope for.) Some of you are going to accomplish great things and become well-known. Some of you have incredible God-given gifts and talents that you need to pursue. But you must purpose to do so.

When God led the Israelites into the land of milk and honey, He did not bottle-feed them; no, someone had to milk the cow and gather the honey. You can be assured that someone got stung by a bee in the process. They still had to work to gather their blessings. And so it is with you: You are going to have to work for your dreams. You are going to have to make it happen.

You must believe in yourself. Do not look back on your past or let it hinder you from changing your life. Said another way, do not let your past dictate your future. It does not matter what your family history is; you can excel if you want to. To accomplish this, you must change your thinking to line up with your dreams. Like Joyce Meyers says, "Get rid of the stinking thinking"—it will only hold you back. Know that you are going to keep on going and that you will never give up. Press on toward the goal.

When I was a small boy, we had a black-and-white TV with a rabbit-ear antenna. We had a record player and an AM radio in our car. Personal computers were not even invented, and we had not yet been to the moon. Today we have satellite TV, remote controls, FM radio, digital and satellite broadcasting worldwide. Record players turned into eight-tracks, then cassettes, then CDs, and now digital electronic devices like iPods. Computers are everywhere. I have one in my car and one in my house, a portable laptop, and even a computer in my watch. Yes, even my scuba-diving watch is computerized! After a dive, I can download the information into my computer and analyze my dive. And today we have people living in space, in space stations.

Why do I share all of this? Because I believe that you and your generation will see even greater discoveries than I have over the last many years. You are in a generation of great change in our world. You will not only see and experience these great discoveries, inventions, and world changes, *you will be a part of them*. Some of you will influence our world and be at the very heart of it all.

Around the year 2000, our world's population reached 6 billion people. Today we are at approximately 6.7 billion. We are projected to reach 9 billion people within the next thirty years. With this population explosion will come many advances in the human race, and you will be right in the middle of it. I challenge you to go forth and make your mark. Go and be all you can be! I believe that you can accomplish the miraculous with God's help. You can live a life of great blessings. Go for it!

Time to Make a U-TURN

Before you can go in the right direction, you must first acknowledge that your life is headed in the wrong direction. Admitting this fact is critical. Without this admission, you'll think you are just fine. Once you have admitted to yourself that you need change, decide what you want to change and what your new destination and goals are.

Now, start working on it. You must line up your daily routine with the destination you have in mind. Think about it: Say you have decided to make something out of your life, and you have a goal in mind. Are your actions today helping you take baby steps toward your desired destination in life, or are they driving you farther away from your dreams? If you are not moving closer to your dreams, you are going to have to make some changes—so why not start right now?

To help you down this road, I have included a section in chapter 9 to help you plan out your goals and a format to write out your road map (your Action Plan) to accomplishing your goals and dreams—so read on.

Learn from Those Who Have Gone Before You

One goal of every Christian is to become more Christlike. When I was working in the corporate world, I went to a seminar on how to become successful, and they had some very good advice. They told us to take a look at someone who was successful and purpose to follow his or her example. Get to know this person; find out what worked for him and what did not. In other words, learn from those who have gone before you.

If you have had a drug or alcohol problem and you go right back to the same crowd doing the same old thing, it won't take long for you to fall right back into the same old stuff. Think about it: if you are trying to beat alcoholism, you don't hang out at the bar. If you are trying to beat a drug problem, you don't hang out with drug dealers and drug users. That's right: you are going to have to start some new habits, and most likely with some new friends, at least until you are strong enough to say "no." Realistically, this can take a very long time.

Do Spiritual Surgery

Some people are delivered from their addictions instantly and never go back to them; others are delivered over a period of time. That is how it was with me. It was a process that took a while. As I look back, I see one major Turning Point. So let me tell you how it went for me.

After my wife and I were married, our house became the party house. Every night, our friends would come over and party. It never stopped. I remember one night that got a little out of hand. When we awoke the next morning, we discovered the house had been destroyed. The sofa back was broken and lying flat on the ground. One of our friends was so sick from too much alcohol that he sat there on the sofa, vomiting on himself. Fortunately, some helpful pal constructed a barf chute out of cardboard and gave him an empty ice chest as a barf tank. On the other sofa was another friend, passed out with a jar of peanut butter on his lap and peanut butter all over him. Apparently he had been eating the peanut butter out of the jar with his bare hands. The refrigerator was wide open, and every last bite of food was gone. Sound fun? Maybe it was at first, but it got old quick.

My new wife decided that she'd had enough of our lifestyle. One day, she said that this was not what she had expected our marriage to be like. She told me I needed to choose the crazy party life with my friends or the married life with her.

Since I loved her so much, I chose the married life. That Turning Point saved me. We moved and changed our phone number and did not tell anyone where we'd gone. We started attending church on a regular basis. It still took me a long time to quit partying altogether, but our move got me away from the hardcore partyers immediately, and our life took an instant turn for the better.

The same principle goes for you. If you want a change in your life, you are going to have to make some adjustments. Do spiritual surgery. You cannot keep doing the same things over and over again and expect different results. No, if you want different results in your life, you need to start doing different things and maybe even hanging out with different people. If you want to be a gangbanger, then hang out with gangbangers; but if you want to live a blessed and prosperous Christian life, then start hanging out with blessed, prosperous Christians. It's not rocket science. You can do it!

If your situation is desperate, you may have to make radical changes.

In John 5, there's a story of a lame man Jesus healed. Jesus told him, "Stand up, pick up your mat, and walk!" Instantly the man was healed. He rolled up his mat and began walking. Then Jesus told him, "Now that you are well, stop sinning, or something even worse may happen to you." Did you catch that? He basically told him that he needed to do a U-TURN away from his current lifestyle, because apparently it was one of destruction.

You are standing at a crossroads today. It's now time for your life to change. Decide where you want to go, make a U-TURN if you have to, learn from others, and do spiritual surgery if you need it.

Afraid that all these things won't be enough? Maybe they won't—by themselves. Before we go any further, it's time to face the greatest Turning Point of your life: an encounter with Jesus Christ.

This is what the crossroads is *really* all about.

Important Points

1. Is your life going in the wrong direction? God allows U-TURNs.
2. Line up your direction with your desired destination.
3. You have to purpose to get where you want to be in life.
4. You are going to have to work on gathering in your blessings and accomplishing your dreams. You are going to have to make it happen.
5. Do not let your past dictate your future. You can succeed if you really want to.
6. Get rid of any stinking thinking.
7. Tell yourself that you can do it and that you will never give up.
8. An encounter with Jesus Christ is what the crossroads is really all about. It's time!

Part 2

Standing at the Crossroads

Chapter 6

Restoration

THE MOST IMPORTANT THING you can do if you want to see your life change is to encounter Jesus Christ and put your life in His hands. He can Reverse the Curse in your life! In this section, we'll look at how to encounter Christ. It begins with repentance (a U-TURN) and restoration (a relationship). From there, we'll go into the Thirty-Day Challenge, and you'll really learn what it means to walk in the power of God!

You should know that even though I drank alcohol as much as I did, I still read my Bible and prayed. You see, that is what I was taught in Sunday school. My deliverance from alcohol came after I decided to seek more of God. I researched every scripture I could find dealing with alcohol. I made a list of these scriptures and read them daily for a long time. As long as I was attending worship services on a regular basis, I was OK. When I missed church, I sometimes slipped. So the Lord told me that in order to overcome, I needed to be in church as often as possible. I started attending worship services on Sunday morning, Sunday night, and Wednesday night. Thank you, Jesus, I am free from alcoholism and all other drugs today.

Today I am clean and sober. My wife and I have been married over twenty-five years. We have three beautiful children and three grandchildren, and the Lord has birthed an evangelistic outreach ministry through us called Restoration Ministries. The Lord has used this ministry to bless many people in different ways. It has been blessed by the Lord to help provide in excess of one million meals through grocery distribution, and it has provided clothes, blankets, help with utility bills, and help finding jobs and cars. In addition, we have seen a few hundred people accept Jesus as their Lord and Savior, thus helping them turn toward blessings and turn their back on curses. This is what we call restoration.

Repentance: U-TURN Away from Curses!

Restoration begins with repentance: making a U-TURN toward God, away from curses and toward blessings. You too can make a U-TURN in life. As my wife's bumper sticker says, "If you don't like the direction your life is going, God allows U-TURNs." Think about it. If you are one who is tempted to party with your friends, or especially if you are already using alcohol and drugs, you may be headed for disaster. Why would you think you are exempt from the hurts this lifestyle can and often does lead to? Or maybe you are not into drugs, but you are into some other sin-related activity, like gangbanging or witchcraft. You might think it is cool; you might think it is fun. Let me tell you, that is a deception! What looks good on the outside and appears to taste as sweet as honey is just in disguise. In the end, it will sting with deadly venom. When they are in your body, sin and addictions can poison you until they bring a life of curses: death and destruction to you and your children.

Yes, the Bible talks about generational curses too. How you live your life can affect your descendants! In the book of Deuteronomy 5:9–10, the Lord told the Israelites, "For I the Lord your God am a jealous God, punishing the children for the sin of the fathers to the third and fourth generation of those who hate me, but showing love to a thousand generations of those who love me and keep my commandments" (NIV). Have you ever noticed that some things seem to run in families? If the parents are always broke, busted, and disgusted, oftentimes the kids will live the same life. On the other hand, if the parents live an abundant life full of blessings and prosperity, oftentimes their children will do the same. I think this is often because of generational blessings or generational curses. Think about it. How you live your life can affect your kids and grandkids!

Are you ready for a new direction in your life, a U-TURN? I've written my own definition of *U-TURN* for this book:

> A U-TURN is a complete reversal in the direction your life is going—a course correction away from a lifestyle of hurt, addictions, and trouble toward a life of hope, restoration, blessings, prosperity, and a future. It is turning defeat into victory, tragedy into triumph. It is turning your troubles into your testimony. It stands for rebuilding and restoring your relationships with family and friends. It is all about taking a different path in life that leads to your success in God's eyes with God's help and an eternity in heaven.

In doing a U-TURN, you can Reverse the Curse. Just because your parents lived a non-Christian life does not mean you have to live with the burden of suffering from their poor choices. Here is the deal: the Bible says in Ezekiel 18:19–20 that if a son does "what is just and right and has been careful to keep all my decrees, he will surely live . . . The son will not share the guilt of the father" (NIV). Put in today's terms: if you will repent of your sins, accept Jesus as your personal Savior and live for Him, He will forgive your sins and you can Reverse the Curse. You will no longer have to let your past or your family's past dictate your future.

Restoration: Answer the Call of Christ!

The Bible says that "God so loved the world that he gave his one and only Son, that whoever believes in him shall not perish but have eternal life. For God did not send his Son into the world to condemn the world, but to save the world through him" (John 3:16–17, NIV).

If you are ready for that change in your life and you have never accepted Jesus as your personal Savior, you can do so today.

Jesus is inviting you now: "Here I am! I stand at the door and knock. If anyone hears my voice and opens the door, I will come in and eat with him and he with me" (Revelation 3:20, NIV).

All, every single one of you is invited! "Everyone who calls on the name of the Lord will be saved" (Romans 10:13, NIV).

> Salvation is a free gift.
> *"The gift of God is eternal life in Christ Jesus our Lord"*
> *(Romans 6:23, NIV).*

You can have assurance of salvation. "To all who receive Him, to those who believe in His name, He gives the right to become children of God" (John 1:12, NIV).

Receive salvation today. "If you confess with your mouth 'Jesus is Lord,' and believe in your heart that God raised Him from the dead, you are saved. For it is with your heart that you believe and are justified, and it is with your mouth that you confess and are saved" (Romans 10:9–10 NIV).

Why do you need salvation, you might ask? Because all have sinned and fallen short of the glory of God (Romans 3:23), and the wages of sin is death (Romans 6:23). You've already seen where bad choices can lead. Now it's time to turn toward Christ.

To ask Jesus into your life, simply say:

Jesus, I believe that You are the Son of God and that You died on the cross for me. Please forgive me of my sins and come into my heart. Jesus, I receive You this day as my personal Lord and Savior. Help me now to live for You day by day. Thank You, Jesus. Amen.

Now that you have accepted Jesus into your life, you must trust in Him!

Proverbs 3:5–6 says, "Trust in the Lord with all of your heart and lean not on your own understanding: in all your ways acknowledge him and he will make your paths straight" (NIV).

This means to trust and acknowledge God in *all* your ways, in everything you do, in all aspects of your life. Do this, and your life will change. Seek to know more of God and His ways. I believe with all my heart that if you will pursue a relationship with the Lord God Almighty with sincere passion, it will be the beginning of your new life. To help you do this in a life-changing way, it's time for the Thirty-Day Challenge.

Important Points
1. How you live your life can affect your children and grandchildren.
2. Salvation is a free gift.
3. If you confess with your mouth Jesus is Lord and believe in your heart that God raised Him from the dead, you are saved.
4. If you will pursue a relationship with the Lord God Almighty with sincere passion, it will be the beginning of your new life.

Chapter 7

The Thirty-Day Challenge

WHEN YOU DESPERATELY WANT and need change in your life, you can do it. You will need to start with the help of the God of All Creation. In the next two chapters, you'll learn how to do the Thirty-Day Challenge—and how it can change your life.

What Is the Thirty-Day Challenge?

The Thirty-Day Challenge is a personal pledge of total commitment to begin the process of change in your life with God's help in passionate pursuit of Him with all your heart through prayer, study of the Holy Bible, worship in song, and fellowship with other Christians for thirty days.

How to Do the Thirty-Day Challenge

To complete the Thirty-Day Challenge successfully, you have to plan for it. First and foremost, you have to make the time. Schedule it! It must take priority over TV, the Internet, hobbies, sports, and anything else that distracts you. The more you put into it, the more you will get out of it. This is no half-hearted effort! If you are not willing to give the challenge your best effort, you may not want change badly enough. If you are desperate for change, you will go for it.

1. Get a small calendar book and schedule your day. Schedule your time with God. You will need to spend more time in pursuit of your relationship with God than ever before in your life.

2. Give it all you can for thirty days. The more you put into it, the more you will get out of it. Target spending at least one hour per day praying and reading your Bible. Keep a logbook and write notes, recording what the Lord is speaking to you through your prayers and study of His Word, the Holy Bible.

3. Make it a priority. You can count on life's distractions to come your way, so plan on saying "no." During these thirty days, you have to be able to tell people that you are involved in the process of change in your life. It is a priority, and your schedule is full right now.

4. Find a Jesus-preaching, full-Bible Christian church that loves to worship God with live music, and go every time the doors are open. Go to all the functions. Be bold in meeting Christians: they will help you on your journey. Be open and honest.

5. Set up reminders in places you frequent every day. A post-it on your bathroom mirror saying "I CAN DO THIS" or a note on your workspace that says "THIRTY-DAY CHALLENGE" can help keep you on track. I like to post scriptures that say "I am more than a conqueror with God's help" or "I can do all things through Christ Jesus who strengthens me."

6. Carry a reminder for the entire thirty days. I have a medallion with a special motivational message on it. What can you carry as a reminder? Try finding a penny made the year you were born. Carry it always. Every time you see it, read the inscription: "In God We Trust." When you are faced with temptation or a difficult time, hold it in your hand and pray for God's strength. If you are in public, you can pray silently in your head. The idea is to set your heart and thoughts on the God of All Creation in all areas of your life during these thirty days.

I challenge you to do this faithfully for just thirty days. If you do so with sincere intentions of drawing closer to your Lord and Savior Jesus, I guarantee you will. The Bible says in Jeremiah 29:13, "'When you seek me with your whole heart I will be found by you and I will restore you' declares the Lord" (NIV). This could be the beginning of your new life.

Changing Your Lifestyle for Thirty Days—and Beyond

You can do it! You can overcome the temptations of drugs, alcohol, and a partying lifestyle. To do so, you will need to read your Bible and pray daily. Make it a routine. The best time for me is when I first wake up in the morning. In fact, I try to get up an hour early each day to pray and read the written Word of God, the Bible.

I suggest that you first read the Gospel of John. Then start in Matthew, and read the entire New Testament or as far as you can get in thirty days. Again, if you do this with sincere intentions to draw closer to your Lord and Savior—you will!

In addition, you will need to plug into a Bible-based, Jesus-seeking church. You will need this Christian fellowship. Seek out a church that loves to worship our Lord and Savior Jesus, Son of God, King of Kings, and does so with great enthusiasm.

This will be a place you can go for encouragement and teaching. It will fill your spiritual gas tank. And when you go out into the world and your tank gets low, you need to come back and fill it up. I found that until I built the inner strength to overcome drunkenness, I needed church Sunday morning, Sunday night, and Wednesday night. It gave me the fuel, the strength to overcome the temptation. Hebrews 10:25 says, "We should not forsake the assembling of one another" (NIV). It says this because we need to be around other Christians on a regular basis.

Paul tells us to be imitators of God as dear children (Ephesians 5:1). We should heed his instruction and earnestly desire to be like Jesus in every way. Find someone who is a successful Christian, as evidenced by the fruit he or she produces, and get to know this person, learn his way and follow her example. This is a great way to live the Christian life successfully. The most important factor in learning to become Christlike, however, is to know what it means to be just that. What is Christ like? This you must do through learning the Word of God. Once you begin to learn the Word of God and get it inside you, you will begin to be transformed from the inside out. Soon your outward fruit will be apparent.

This last January, my wife and I resolved to take the Thirty-Day Challenge once again. We were seeking God for direction in the new year and just wanting more of Him. We committed to spend more time pursuing God each day than ever before in our lives. We worshiped Him in song, and we prayed and read our Bibles every day, sometimes for hours. The result was incredible. God's Word is true, and it proves itself over and over throughout the ages. It says in several places that if you will chase after God with all your heart, with sincere motives, putting Him first above everything else, you will draw closer to Him. Our spiritual sensitivity was greatly increased during those thirty days, and we have a renewed zeal to serve Him and do His will.

No matter who you are or what your relationship is with our Lord and Savior, if you will step up your passion and pursuit of God, you will experience more of Him. If you already read your Bible for fifteen minutes a day, read it for thirty minutes or an hour. Do you pray daily? Step it up: pray two, three, or four times longer. Pray with passion, and believe that what you ask will be answered. Do you worship Him in songs and hymns daily? If not, start now. The more you put into your relationship with God, the more you will get out of it. This is a Bible promise, or as I like to refer to it, a spiritual law. The Holy Bible says it, and it is true.

During our Thirty-Day Challenge, it became impressed in my spirit that we needed to make this passionate pursuit of God a routine part of our lives, not just for a set number of days. We have become a watered-down, lazy group of people when it comes to seeking God, to actually serving Him and doing His will! Revelation 2:4–5 basically says to the church, "Repent, you lazy people, and return to doing the works of God as one returns to his first love." Prayer can change things. If you really want to experience God during this Thirty-Day Challenge, you have got to spend much time seeking Him and praying. You cannot be lazy about it. Think of it like this: the Thirty-Day Challenge you are about to participate in can be the beginning of a new life for you—so give it all you possibly can.

During our Thirty-Day Challenge, I felt like the Holy Spirit revealed to me one of the secrets contained in the holy scriptures. (It is not really a secret, but most of us do not tap into it.) Many mighty moves of God were started with one person on his or her knees in diligent, sincere, passionate prayer. This challenge too can be the beginning of a mighty move of God in your life, so plan on spending much time in prayer.

I share all of this with you in an effort to help you understand the importance of prayer in your efforts to change. If you want to change, commit to the Thirty-Day Challenge, and you will see a difference—*if* you do it with a sincere heart and really pour yourself into it with passionate, devoted zeal for more of God in your life.

I am not talking about periodic, halfhearted prayer. I am talking about an everyday commitment with all of your heart. The more you put into it, the more you will get out of it.

Do You Really Want This?

If you are struggling with destructive habits, drugs, or alcohol, you need to start the Thirty-Day Challenge. The question is, do you want it badly enough?

I have been corresponding with a man in jail. He is twenty-seven years old and has two children. He tells me that he has been using drugs, primarily crank, since he was thirteen. His parents also used the drug (they called it "bathtub dope," because some people make it at home in a bathtub), and it was hard not to use it when Mom and Dad were doing it. This stuff is nasty; I have used it as well. I can remember laying in a corner feeling like my heart was going to explode, wondering if I had used too much crank and if I was going to die. It is a terrible feeling that most crank users have experienced.

This man tells me about how much he loves his children and how he would do anything for them. He says he has tried over and over to stop using, but something is always there to interfere. He admits that he is weak and that he needs help. He now acknowledges that he must not move back to his old neighborhood, where the crank is available at a moment's notice. He says he is tired of living this life, but he is weak and he needs help. Here is a section from one of his letters.

Dear Fred,

First of all I want to apologize for not writing you sooner. I had a conflict with another inmate and now I've cost myself fifteen days in the hole. So any-hoo, I read your story and I liked it very much and relate to a lot of it. I don't know how much you know about me, but I'll tell you a little about myself.

I am twenty-seven years old and started do-ing drugs at the age of thirteen and haven't been able to put them away yet. I started my first drug with crank. My mom and dad used to make it; they called it bathtub dope. And from there it led onto other drugs.

I'm a father of two, one daughter who is three years old, and a son who is soon to be two years old. And I love them so dearly I'd do anything in the world for them. I've tried and tried to stop us-ing drugs, but something is always there to inter-fere with that, and I'm willing to admit that I'm very weak at stopping (quitting).

This last time before I got arrested I actually was trying and doing my best. I was working every day, and on the weekends I'd either spend my time with my kids or go fishing with my cousins. They're (were) my only support out there, now one is dead and the other is relearning how to speak and walk. It all happened from a drunk driver. They were very close cousins, I guess you could say we were best friends. We grew up with each other. I lost it and went back to using and got caught up on a parole violation facing six years in prison.

I'm tired, I can't go on living this kind of life, I need help and guidance. All I know how to live is either high or three free meals and a cot between four solid walls. I'm ready to change my ways in life. I've been trying to read the Bible but there is a lot of old-fashioned words that I just don't understand, and when I was put here in the hole they took all my books including my Bible that I had, and when I asked for another one they handed me the Book of Mormon. But I don't believe in the Mormon ways, I think they're messin' with me. But for now I'll stick with the scriptures that you have given me, for they are very helpful, and please, if and when you have time, please send me more that will help keep my spirits up. Thank you for taking the time to show me that I do have another chance in life. I hope to hear back from you soon.

Thank you! Much Respect.

This man is just one of millions suffering a life of destruction because of his drug addictions. And like many, many others, he has tried over and over again to stop without success. His letter speaks of addictions that were passed on to him by his parents: some call this generational curses. He also tells about how his cousin and best friend is dead due to a drunk driver. I hope you understand now why I say drugs and alcohol will ruin your life. They can ruin your family and lead to death, destruction, and an eternity in the burning flames of hell.

If you are like this man and you are locked up, you can still start the process of changing your life. You should have the time to take the Thirty-Day Challenge to a new level.

Get your hands on a Holy Bible and determine to read the whole Bible. Start with the New Testament; when you finish it, read the entire Old Testament. You may not finish the whole Bible in thirty days, but keep going until you are finished. Take notes as you go. Write down the scriptures that seem to pertain to you. If you can get your hands on a colored highlighter, highlight these scriptures.

Set your heart on memorizing the scriptures that give you strength to be an overcomer. I personally think that every believer should memorize Psalm 91: it is awesome! Getting God's Word in your memory will help you get it in your heart and spirit. Memorizing scripture will give you guidance for life and help you change from the old you to a new life. When I lived in California, I had a good friend and ministry partner who was saved in prison. He joined our ministry team and eventually became a chaplain for jail ministry. You too can change your life.

Important Points
1. The Bible says that when you seek God with your whole heart, He will be found by you and He will restore you.
2. Once you begin to learn the Word of God and get it inside you, you will begin to be transformed from the inside out. Soon your outward fruit will be apparent.
3. This challenge too can be the beginning of a mighty move of God in your life, so plan on spending much time in prayer.

Chapter 8

Beating the Challenges to the Challenge

IF YOU SET OUT TO COMPLETE the Thirty-Day Challenge, you can bet that your enemy the devil will set out to challenge you. In this chapter, we'll look at how to overcome his attacks when they come. This advice will work not only in the Thirty-Day Challenge, but throughout your life. If you are reading this for a friend who is struggling to overcome addiction in his or her life, there is advice here for you too. Keep reading!

First, to overcome the challenges that will come your way, you need to read your Bible daily. I once heard someone say, "Dusty Bibles cause dirty lives." Think about it. What is your strength to live a good life? Don't be fooled: it is not your own ability! The Bible teaches us that when we are in relationship with Jesus, we can accomplish many great things, but when we are not in relationship with Him, we are like a branch from a fruit tree that is cut off and dried up. It cannot bear fruit unless it is attached to the tree (see John 15:4–6).

Another one of our problems is that we suffer from a lack of knowledge. The Bible says that we are in a battle: not one of flesh and blood, but a spiritual battle.

> For we wrestle not against flesh and blood, but against principalities, against powers, against the rulers of the darkness of this world, against spiritual wickedness in high places. Wherefore take unto you the whole armour of God, that ye may be able to withstand in the evil day, and having done all, to stand. (Ephesians 6:12–13, KJV)

Ephesians 6 goes on to say that our principal offensive weapon is the Sword of the Spirit, which is the Word of God. When you have the Word of God within you, the Holy Spirit will bring it to your thoughts when you need it. Last week, I was talking to a gentleman about the Lord, and it was as if the words just flowed from my inner being. It was a supernatural experience. His life had been up and down, mostly down, and he decided to accept Jesus as his personal Savior right then and there.

Jesus, when tempted of Satan, used the Word of God as His weapon by responding several times with, "It is written . . ." When you are faced with life's trials and tribulations—you know, the storms we all seem to go through—remember the scripture that fits the situation. Say it aloud, and it will give you strength to overcome.

When I relocated my family to Idaho, I started my own business. It was a major change from working in the corporate world for twenty years. I found myself doing all kinds of physically demanding work outside, in temperatures below freezing. There were two scriptures I repeated over and over that got me through. The first was, "I can do all things through Christ which strengtheneth me" (Philippians 4:13, KJV), and the other was, "Not by might, nor by power, but by my spirit, saith the LORD" (Zechariah 4:6, KJV).

As I spoke these scriptures out loud, it was like I found new strength from within to keep on going. The Holy Bible also gives us instructions for everyday life. Some people like to say that B.I.B.L.E. stands for "Basic Instructions Before Leaving Earth." It does in fact give us clear, basic instructions for life. We often want to pray about something when it is already clear what the answer is. For example, we want something that we cannot afford. Instead of saving up so we can buy it, we say "Let's pray about buying it now." If we know the Word of God, we already know that it says to owe no man anything, but we don't like that answer, so we say "Let's pray about it," and somehow we justify buying something we really do not need on credit. So read your Bible daily and memorize many scriptures: this will give you power for living. The man who wrote that letter from prison stated that he is ready to change his life and that he needs help and guidance.

For Friends and Family

Often, we don't get to a point where we are really ready to make the change until our family gets burned out on us and says, "That is it! We are done trying to help you—when you really get your act together, by proof of your actions, then and only then will we help you."

If you are one of those family members or friends, please let me encourage you, *do not give up on your loved one*. Seek counseling; talk to others about what you can do to help your family member or friend out of this lifestyle. I can relate. I have had close friends and family with these issues who just seemed to take advantage, who never change year after year.

You can help in ways that will not enable your loved one to continue down this path to destruction. For example, if you know that you cannot give him money because he will not spend it wisely, then don't. Instead, help him get the help he needs to overcome his addictions. Read on, and take to heart the suggestions contained in this book as a road map to a new life.

Like the man who wrote the letter in the last chapter, millions of Americans need help and guidance. What they do not need is help to stay a drunk and a drug addict. Often, people think they are helping by giving money to someone struggling with these addictions because of the outward appearances: no food, no money, no ability to pay the rent, kids in need, and so on. But these conditions are often the *effects* of this destructive lifestyle, not the cause. The cause is often the addictions, and the cause of the addictions may be an even deeper layer.

If you just give an addicted person money, most likely he or she will spend it on drugs and alcohol, and not on food or paying the bills. Instead of giving cash, meet the need head-on. If you want to help with food, go and buy the food and take it to your friend. If you want to help with the heating or electricity bill, then take your friend down there and pay it with him. If he or she needs help getting off the drugs and alcohol, then help with that. How, you ask?

There are many suggestions in this book for you to follow, but one really helpful way is to find a support group, like Celebrate Recovery, at your local Christian church, and take your friend to it. That's right—if you care enough about your friend, you will take him. I don't mean provide the transportation and drop him off; no, I mean go *with* him. Sit next to your friend and support him or her all the way. You might be surprised: you might learn something too!

Celebrate Recovery is in Christian churches all across America. It is Christian-based, and you should be able to get help from these people. (Note: Not all groups have the same dynamics. Look for one that has been meeting for a while and is established. The Celebrate Recovery group I take a friend to serves dinner for free if you cannot afford the $3 fee and provides free childcare.)

Another way to help your loved one is to help with spiritual surgery. In a nutshell, this is to help addicts separate from addictions and the people and things that cause them to participate in addictive activities.

Important Points

1. If you set out to complete the Thirty-Day Challenge, you can bet that your enemy the devil will set out to challenge you.
2. In order to overcome temptations, you will need to read your Bible and pray daily. Make it a scheduled routine.
3. Memorize many scriptures from the Holy Bible: this will give you power for living.
4. Never give up on a friend or family member. Seek help; talk to others about how you can help your loved one out of this destructive lifestyle. Help in a way that will not enable him or her to continue down the path to destruction.

Part 3

Beyond the Crossroads:

Living Your New Life

Chapter 9

Cast Your Net on the Other Side: Make an Action Plan!

THE GOSPEL OF JOHN RECORDS that after Jesus was crucified and rose from the dead, He appeared to His disciples on various occasions. On one of these occasions, the disciples had been fishing all night and had caught nothing. Standing on the beach, Jesus yelled out to them, "Friends, haven't you caught any fish?" They shouted, "No!" Jesus told them to cast their nets on the other side of the boat—and they hauled in an enormous catch.

To paraphrase what Jesus is saying, "If you're not catching any fish where you always go fishing, find a new fishing spot or cast your net in different waters." Applying this principle to your life, if you are not happy with the results your life is producing, if you are not happy with what you are catching in the same old fishing hole—it is time to make some changes!

Cast your net in different waters. Come on now: If you are tired of going to jail because you keep getting caught stealing for a living, it is time for a change. Cast your net into new waters—get a haircut and a real job. You can do it. I know that I have touched on this theme previously, but it is critical that you get this.

> *If you want to change your life for the better, you are going to have to* purpose *to improve it.*

When my wife and I decided we wanted to get away from the crazy party crowd, we had to take drastic action. We had to move, change our phone numbers, and totally disassociate ourselves from those who were doing things we wanted to get away from. It is not rocket science: if you want to change any area of your life, you must take action. I had to make the decision. Did I want the party life with my friends, or did I want the married life with my wife, whom I loved with all my heart? There I was, standing at a crossroads in my life. I chose the married life, and I am glad I did.

Today I have three grown children and three grandchildren. I love them all so very much. I cannot imagine my life without any of them. Often I think of those party buddies of mine—some of them made it, but many of them did not. What do you want to change in your life? How badly do you want it? Decide what it is and do it. You can make it if you want it badly enough and never give up. Remember what I had to do to stop drinking? It was hard, but I did it.

My daughter Stephanie was at a crossroads in her life. She was in her last year of high school and had started hanging around with friends who were partyers. She had been involved in the youth group at church, and she knew better. Yet the deceptive pull of this lifestyle is intriguing at first. It seems sweet as honey, but when you get in the middle of it, it sours your stomach and can ruin your life. My daughter needed to make a choice.

Stephanie made the decision to enroll in the intern program at Capital Christian Center in Boise, Idaho, and it transformed her life. She is now on staff at the church as administrator of the youth group, and she oversees the small groups for high-school girls. She just got back from her second missionary trip to Africa, and she has been to the White House in support of the National Prayer Center in Washington DC to pray with our nation's leaders. She knew she wanted to take a different direction in life, and she took the steps to change. You too can transform your life—*if* you will work on it and never give up.

This "cast your net on the other side" principle applies to any area of your life. It applies to *all* of you: your business, your church, and so on. I have seen people who are highly educated, with master's and doctorate degrees, who desperately wanted to change something in their lives, their businesses, or their churches, and yet they were unable to do so. It's not that they didn't have the knowledge. In fact, some of these people can teach others the steps in the process of change—yet they lack the ability to follow through. No matter who you are, you can change your life for the better if you will just commit to making it happen. Talking about it or reading books is not enough. You must follow through. You can't keep doing the same things over and over again and expect different results.

In summary, to begin living your new life, figure out what you need to do differently and do it. In order to help you through this process, I have included my own version of a road map for accomplishing a goal in your life. I call it the Action Plan. This is a simple planning process that will help you identify your goal, outline the steps needed to accomplish your goal, plan it out, and go for it.

Get a Sponsor

I highly recommend that you partner with someone to help you stay focused and on track. Let's call this person your sponsor. Without answering to someone else, it's easy to just give up when times get tough. I think of my own exercise schedule: When I have a workout partner, I am diligent in my routine. However, if it's just me, I seldom stick to it for any length of time because I have no one to answer to. If you are tired of the lifestyle you have been living and you desperately want to do a U-TURN and change the direction your life is headed, then you must find accountability.

I recommend a Christian-based group called Celebrate Recovery. Celebrate Recovery groups meet on a regular basis to support each other. Get out the phone book, call the churches in your area, and ask if they have a Celebrate Recovery program. Ask to speak to the leader of the group in person. Go, explain your situation, and ask the leader to recommend someone to meet with you on a regular basis. Explain that you have an Action Plan. Share it and ask for feedback. The Bible says that a wise man seeks many counselors. Take to heart any feedback, and adjust your Action Plan if you feel led to do so.

Other potential sponsors might be trusted Christian friends, the pastor of a church, or the ministry leader of a men's or women's group at church. You will see how valuable this accountability partner can be as we get into the Action Plan itself.

If you are a person with a major vision or goal, having an accountability partner can greatly increase your chances of success with this type of goal mapping. All too often I have seen people set goals with great visions and fail to accomplish them. Another mistake is to choose someone as a sponsor who will not give you open and honest feedback. This often happens when a very strong-willed person asks a weaker-willed person to sponsor him or her. If you are one of these people, you really need a neutral party to be your accountability partner, someone who is willing and able to be open and honest and tell you the truth. Remember, you desperately need change in your life. Find someone who will tell it like it is but who really cares about you making it.

The idea is to share your goals with someone who can help keep you accountable. Without accountability or consequences for failure, most people fall short.

Starting Your Action Plan
Let's get started.
In general, to make an Action Plan you will:

1. Write down a specific goal you want to accomplish.

2. Identify all the steps to accomplish that goal.

3. Prioritize each step.

4. Calendarize the steps, with due dates for each one.

5. Publish your Action Plan: do not keep it a secret.

6. Select a sponsor or accountability partner and share your Action Plan.

7. Decide on frequency to meet with your sponsor.

8. Decide on any accountability guidelines.

Instructions for Creating Your Action Plan
1. Develop your goal statement, and be specific.
You are not trying to impress anyone with a fancy statement that can be posted on a wall. Unfortunately, this is what happens to most so-called "Vision Statements"—they get posted somewhere, and in actuality they mean nothing. Not yours. Your goal statement is not only what you want to accomplish,

but what you desperately need to do to change your life. Don't get caught up in the game of "Will others be impressed with it?" No, you must ask yourself, what does this mean to me?

Here are some examples of a goal statement:

- I will beat the drug and alcohol addiction in my life, make new, sober friends, and become a successful, healthy, prosperous person with God's help.
- My life will do a U-TURN away from my destructive habits and addictions. I will become blessed and highly favored. With God's help I will restore my family and become a helper to those who have struggled with the same issues.

2. Identify the necessary steps to accomplish your goal.

Think about this carefully, and write down your ideas. Be honest, for you are trying to change your life, not impress anyone. Everyone's situation is different, but your list might look something like this:

- Stay away from people who drag me down.
- Stay away from the partyers in my life.
- Change my phone number.
- Move.
- Get professional help.
- Join a Christian support group like Celebrate Recovery.
- Start going to a Christian church.
- Find Christian friends to hang out with.
- Find a sponsor or accountability partner.
- Read every scripture in the Bible that speaks about drugs and alcohol.

Depending on how bad your situation is, you may need to do spiritual surgery. For example, if you have roommates and there are drugs and alcohol in your house every day, you need to move to get away from it. Sometimes others can suggest things you need to do. I remember my parents and others telling me not to hang around those crazy friends of mine. They said, "You will only get in trouble, and they will drag you down." They were right. A probation officer once told me that my alcohol usage was causing me problems and that was why I was in his office. My first step in turning from the trouble was to accept the fact that alcohol was causing me problems.

3. Prioritize your list.

To do this, simply put the list in order from one to however many steps there are. Start with first things first.

- Stay away from people who drag me down.
- Stay away from the partyers in my life.
- Read every scripture in the Bible that speaks about drugs and alcohol.
- Join a Christian support group like Celebrate Recovery.
- Start going to a Christian church.
- Find Christian friends to hang out with.
- Find a sponsor or accountability partner.
- Get professional help.
- Change my phone number.
- Move.

4. Set due dates for each item on your list.

Everyone's situation is different, so you must be as aggressive as necessary to make the needed changes in your life in good time. I know a man facing his third felony. If convicted, he could serve up to life in prison. He is now on probation, and if he gets caught using drugs or alcohol or getting into any other trouble while on probation prior to his court hearing, he will get hammered by the court. If I were in his shoes, I would do whatever it takes, today, *right now*, to get away from the source of my trouble.

- Stay away from people who drag me down.
     Due by: Today
- Stay away from the partyers in my life.
     Due by: Today
- Start going to a Christian church.
     Due by: This weekend
- Read every scripture in the Bible that speaks about drugs and alcohol.
     Due by: 3/15/10
- Join a Christian support group like Celebrate Recovery.
     Due by: 3/30/10
- Find Christian friends to hang out with.
     Due by: 4/15/10
- Find a sponsor or accountability partner.
     Due by: 3/15/10
- Get professional help if need be.
     Due by: 4/30/10
- Change my phone number.
     Due by: 3/15/10
- Move.
     Due by: 5/30/10

5. For each item, write out how you think you can accomplish it.

This is the "action" part of your Action Plan. For example, Number 1 on this list is "Stay away from people who drag me down." I had to move and change my phone number to get away from the crazy partyers in my life. What will it take for you?

As you write out your Action Plan, do it in simple terms. Again, this is for you to accomplish your goal, not to impress others. Now, meet with someone you trust and go over it with him or her. Ask for their improvement suggestions. Take any suggestions to heart, and revise accordingly.

OK, now you have a plan. If your accountability partner is the person you reviewed your Action Plan with, then great! You are ready to get going. If not, find someone to fill this role and get started.

You can use this format for simple or complex goals. Your Action Plan can be as simple as the one below and still have a life-changing effect.

ACTION PLAN

Goal: Make new Christian friends who don't drink or take drugs or break the law just for fun.

Steps to Accomplish Goal:

Step 1. I will commit to finding new Christian friends who will encourage me in the right direction.

When: I will start this weekend, 3/29/2010.

How: By going to church instead of out to party.

Step 2. I will find a church that is Bible-based, has a great worship service at least once a week, and that I feel comfortable with.

When: I will start this weekend, 3/29/2010.

How: I will go every Sunday and Wednesday night if they meet midweek until I find the church for me. Then I will be a regular member and stick to it.

Step 3. I will attend all the church functions. It may be difficult at first, but I will do it.

When: I will start this weekend, 3/29/2010.

How: I will get a schedule of all the church functions and go to all of them that apply to me.

Remember, if your situation is desperate, you may have to make radical changes. Change is different for each of us, but for some, radical change is necessary. You may have to move away from the lifestyle you are in, change your phone number, get new friends, and so on. Don't lose sight of your goal! It is better to make the decision to change your life for the better than to live a life of misery. Spiritual surgery may be hard, but it results in a new life.

Some of you are thinking that you will not find new friends. You like the ones you have, and you are going to keep them. Well, maybe that will work for you—but those of you who have reached a point in your life where you know without any doubt that you need to make some drastic changes can relate to what I'm saying. If your life is a disaster and you want to change it, you can! You just need to turn from those things that have been plaguing you. You know what they are.

In my own life, I had hit a low point. I knew I was headed for disaster, so I took drastic action. I had to get away from the party crowd. What is it you need to change in your life? The Bible says in Habakkuk 2 that we should write down our vision and make it plain so that we may run with it—make an Action Plan, and go for it!

"What next?" you may be asking. "How do I really live for Jesus? Can you be more specific?"

I thought you would never ask!

Important Points

1. If you're not happy with what you're catching in the same old fishing hole, it's time to make some changes!

2. When my wife and I decided we wanted to get away from the crazy party crowd, we had to take drastic action. If your situation is bad enough, you too may have to take serious action to initiate the process of positive change in your life.

3. No matter who you are, you can change your life for the better if you will just commit to making it happen. Talking

about it or reading books is not enough. You must follow through.

4. The Bible says in Habakkuk 2 that we should write down our vision and make it plain so that we may run with it. Make an Action Plan and go for it!

Chapter 10

God Has Plans for You

In Jeremiah 29:11–14, it says,

"For I know the plans I have for you," declares the LORD, "plans to prosper you and not to harm you, plans to give you hope and a future. Then you will call upon me and come and pray to me, and I will listen to you. You will seek me and find me when you seek me with all your heart. I will be found by you," declares the LORD, "and will bring you back from captivity." (NIV)

Another way to translate the end of that verse is "I will restore you." God knows the plans He has for you. They include hope and a future. He is telling you here that you need to call upon Him through prayer; you need to seek Him with your whole heart, not just on Sunday. If you will do this, God says He will be found by you and He will restore you.

Repentance, Restoration, and Renewal: They're for You!

Repentance is important. If you have not given your life to God and asked Jesus into your heart, you need to repent to do that. If you're already a Christian but you're not living for God, you need to repent too. Second Timothy 2:22 says, *"Flee the evil desires of youth,* and pursue righteousness, faith, love and peace, along with those who call on the Lord out of a pure heart" (NIV, my emphasis). You know what those evil desires of your youth are. God says to flee from them. They will take you down!

Jeremiah 15:19 promises, "The Lord says: If you repent, I will restore you!" (NIV). If you have not yet done so, get down on your knees and repent for your sins. Ask God to forgive you; ask Jesus to come into your heart. Ask Jesus to give you the strength to sin no more. If you stumble or if you fall back into sin, repent and never give up. Be an overcomer.

If you have previously accepted Jesus as your personal Savior but you have not been living for Him, you need restoration! The Bible gives the directions for a U-TURN in your life. You can do it: just follow these directions. I call them "God's Directions for Our Restoration."

Are you ready to put God before those things in your life that hinder your walk with Him?

God's Directions for Our Restoration
Humble yourself and pray.
Acknowledge your sins to the Lord in prayer.
Cry out to the Lord in repentance.
Seek His face.
Seek Him with all your heart, mind, and soul. Pray and read your Bible daily. Search for Him as you would a hidden treasure. Desire Him as an Olympic athlete desires the gold!
Turn from your wicked ways.
Turn from your sin. Make a U-TURN.

Resist the evil desires of your youth.
Remove those things in your life that are detestable to the Lord.
Do not conform any longer to the pattern of this world, but be transformed by the renewing of your mind.
Renew your covenant.
Renew your commitment to the Lord with all your heart and soul, and rejoice because of it. Write it down and tell a friend. Make it official.

Right now, you can renew your covenant with the Lord. Renew your commitment to serve Him now, and celebrate! Celebrate because you have chosen life. You have chosen blessings, therefore shout with joy, for 2 Chronicles 15:2 says, "The Lord is with you when you are with Him. When you look for Him you will find Him. But if you forsake Him, He will forsake you" (NIV). The Living Bible says that after receiving this message, Israel

> *entered into* a contract to worship only the Lord God of their fathers . . . They shouted out their oath of loyalty to God with trumpets blaring and horns sounding. All were happy for this covenant with God, for they had entered into it with all their hearts and wills, and wanted Him above everything else, and they found Him! And He gave them peace throughout the nation" (2 Chronicles 15:12–15, my emphasis)

You too can have peace in Jesus with an eternal reward.

You Can Be an Overcomer—Forever!

Without God's help, we are doomed to failure by the works of our flesh. The Bible identifies some of these works as envying, murder, drunkenness, immorality, impurity, indecency, idolatry, sorcery, hostility, strife, jealousy, selfishness, a party spirit, carousing, adultery, fornication, uncleanness, erotic lust, idolatry, witchcraft, hatred, wrath, strife, and deviation (see Gal 5:19–21).

By contrast, a person transformed by and consistently dependent on the power of God's Spirit will live according to the traits of God's character because of God's empowerment, just as trees bear fruit according to their own kind. This means that it doesn't matter who you are—you can be an overcomer through the power of God Himself!

Galatians goes on to identify the fruit of God's Holy Spirit that dwells in us after we have repented, turned from our wicked ways and stepped into pursuing God: love, joy, peace, long-suffering, gentleness, goodness, faith, meekness, and temperance. Paul says that if we live in the Spirit, we should also walk in the Spirit (see Galatians 5:18, 22–23.)

> Abide in me, and I in you. As the branch cannot bear fruit of itself, except it abide in the vine; no more can ye, except ye abide in me. I am the vine, ye are the branches: he that abideth in me, and I in him, the same bringeth forth much fruit: for without me ye can do nothing. If a man abide not in me, he is cast forth as a branch, and is withered; and men gather them, and cast them into the fire, and they are burned. (John 15:4–6, KJV)

In the book of Revelation, where God lays out His plans for the end of the world, Jesus Christ says, "I am Alpha and Omega, the beginning and the ending . . . which is, and which was, and which is to come, the Almighty," and, "Do not be afraid. I am the First and the Last. I am the Living One: I was dead, and behold I am alive forever and ever! And I hold the keys of death and Hades." He also says, "He who has an ear let him hear what the

Spirit says to the Churches. To him who overcomes, I will give the right to eat from the tree of life, which is in the paradise of God" (Revelation 1:8, 1:17–18, 2:7, NIV and KJV, my emphasis.)

Jesus has much to say about overcomers in Revelation. Remember, if you have accepted Jesus as your personal Savior and are committed to pursuing God, these scriptures are talking about you!

He who has an ear let him hear what the Spirit says to the churches. *He who overcomes* will not be hurt at all by the second death . . . *To him who overcomes*, I will give some of the hidden manna. I will also give him a white stone with a new name written on it, known only to him who receives it. *To him who overcomes* and does my will until the end, I will give him authority over the nations . . .

He who overcomes will, like them, be dressed in white. I will never blot out his name from the book of life, but will acknowledge his name before my Father and his angels . . . *Him who overcomes* I will make a pillar in the temple of my God. Never again will he leave it. I will write on him the name of my God and the name of the city of my God . . . *To him who overcomes*, I will give the right to sit with me on my throne, just as I overcame and sat down with my Father on his throne. He who has an ear, let him hear what the Spirit says to the churches. (NIV, my emphasis. There is more to this passage than I've quoted here. You can read it all in Revelation 2 and 3.)

The blessings of overcoming are awesome both now and forever! So be an overcomer, and experience God's blessings here on earth and on Judgment Day.

It's Time to Give Your All

As a Christian, you cannot live on the borderline, with one foot in sin and one foot following Jesus. You are either hot or cold; serving Jesus is not a lukewarm condition. You need to totally and completely sell out to Jesus, 100%. You have got to live for Him. Jesus says if you are lukewarm, He will spit you out (see Revelation 3:16). You have got to decide if you are going to do this or not. If you are going for it and you want to change your life, don't be a wimp or a closet Christian.

There is nothing wimpy about being a Christian. Have you read about David in the Bible? He fought a lion, a bear, and an eight-foot giant named Goliath. Goliath was in the Philistine army, and he challenged any man from the armies of Israel, but not one was man enough to face him—except little David. David said, "You dare to insult the name of my God!" Goliath was angry that Israel had sent this little man out to him, and he called David a dog. At that, David ran toward him and conquered Goliath. (Read the whole story in 1 Samuel 17.)

David was no wimp; he was a man's man. Yet he prayed and worshiped God publicly. On one occasion, he was dancing and singing worship songs to the Lord God Almighty in the public square, and this embarrassed his wife to the point that she yelled down from a window above for him to stop it. He was not ashamed to worship his God, and we should not be either. In fact, the Bible warns us against this:

Whosoever therefore shall be ashamed of me and of my words in this adulterous and sinful generation; of him also shall the Son of man be ashamed, when he cometh in the glory of his Father with the holy angels. (Mark 8:38, KJV)

Therefore, when you surrender your heart and life to Jesus, give it all 100%. If your family, friends, and coworkers can see no difference in you, then I question your commitment. Yes, this may be an adjustment at first, but you can do this.

It's About Eternity

The Bible says in Revelation,

> Then I saw a great white throne and him who was seated on it. Earth and sky fled from his presence, and there was no place for them. And I saw the dead, great and small, standing before the throne, and the books were opened. Another book was opened, which is the book of life. The dead were judged according to what they had done as recorded in the books. The sea gave up the dead that were in it, and death and Hades gave up the dead that were in them, and each person was judged according to what he had done. Then death and Hades were thrown into the lake of fire. The lake of fire is the second death. *If anyone's name was not found written in the book of life*, he was thrown into the lake of fire . . .
>
> Then I saw a new heaven and a new earth, for the first heaven and the first earth had passed away, and there was no longer any sea. I saw the Holy City, the new Jerusalem coming down out of heaven from God, prepared as a bride beautifully dressed for her husband. And I heard a loud voice from the throne saying, "Now the dwelling of God is with men, and he will live with them. They will be his people, and God himself will be with them and be their God. He will wipe away every tear from their eyes. There will be no more death or mourning or crying or pain, for the old order of

things has passed away." He who was seated on the throne said, "I am making everything new!" Then he said, "Write this down, for these words are trustworthy and true."

He said to me: "It is done. I am the Alpha and the Omega, the Beginning and the End. To him who is thirsty I will give to drink without cost from the spring of the water of life. *He who overcomes will inherit all this, and I will be his God and he will be my son.*

"But the cowardly, the unbelieving, the vile, the murderers, the sexually immoral, those who practice magic arts, the idolaters and all liars— their place will be in the fiery lake of burning sulfur. This is the second death." (Revelation 20:11–15, 21:1–8, NIV, my emphasis.)

Your commitment to turn from the destructive lifestyle of drugs and alcohol, to make a U-TURN toward a lifestyle of Christianity, not only affects you in the here-and-now but in eternity. In comparison to eternity, the Bible refers to this life on earth as a vapor that is here for a moment and gone the next, or a leaf on a tree that is here today and gone tomorrow as the seasons change. Eternity is for ever and ever; it does not end.

Have you read this far without giving your life to Jesus Christ? Now is the time to change that. This is your greatest Turning Point! I have heard it said that one reason we are here is to determine where we want to spend our eternity. Do we want to spend it in the paradise of God that Jesus went to prepare for us, or in the fiery furnace—the fiery lake of burning sulfur prepared for the devil, his demons, and all those whose names are not found written in the book of life? If you were to die right now, where do you think you would go? Do you know that your name is written in the book of life? If not, you can change that right now. It does not matter what you have done previously: God will forgive you. Get on your knees right now, repent of your sins, and start your new life. You can do this.

I like to imagine the scene on Judgment Day as described in Daniel 7 as well as in the book of Revelation. Using my own words and those from Daniel and Revelation, I would describe it like this:

As I looked, the thrones were set in place, and the Mighty God, the Ancient of Days, took his seat as Judge. His throne was magnificent, like no other before it. Earth and sky fled from his presence. His clothing was the purest white as new snow; the hair of his head was white like wool. Thousands upon thousands attended him; every person who had ever lived since the beginning of time, people from every tribe, tongue, and nation stood before him. Their numbers were more than the sands upon the seashore. Who could count them?

The court was seated, and the books were opened. The devil and his evil demons were on one side. They had stacks of giant books that recorded every sin of every man, every sin that was ever committed since the beginning of time. Their evil presences terrified those standing before the throne who had known better but lived an evil life, those who never got around to accepting Jesus as their personal Savior. It was too late for them now. Others cried out, begging for mercy, yet there were others who stood quietly as if they had complete peace.

The Ancient of Days said, "Silence." His powerful voice was heard from one end of the heavens to the other, like a mighty thunder more powerful than you have ever heard. You could hear a pin drop from that point on. The first person was called to the stand. Satan and his demons proceeded to replay every sin this man had ever committed. There were many. Their case was strong, and it appeared he was headed for the second death—the fiery lake of burning sulfur.

As I looked up, there was one coming with the clouds of heaven: He approached the Ancient of Days. It was the Lamb That Was Slain, Jesus, the Savior of man. His face shone like the sun as if to bring light to the heavens. He had only one book: it was the book of life. Jesus opened the book and found the man's name written in it, and the Ancient of Days slammed His hammer down, proclaiming "Not guilty—case closed." The man was embraced by Jesus and allowed to pass through the pearly gates of heaven into the paradise of God. The devil and his evil demons were furious. They called the next person. Every person who did not have his or her name recorded in the book of life was thrown into the lake of fire. Every person whose name was written in the book of life was embraced by Jesus and entered through the pearly gate, the entrance into heaven, the paradise of God.

After everyone was judged, there was no one left in the courtroom except the Ancient of Days, Jesus, Satan, and his demons. Suddenly, fire came down and devoured Satan and his demons, and they were thrown into the fiery lake of burning sulfur where they will be tormented day and night forever.

Jesus said on the last page of the Bible,

Behold, I am coming soon! My reward is with me, and I will give to everyone according to what he has done. I am the Alpha and the Omega, the First and the Last, The Beginning and the End. Blessed are those who wash their robes, that they may have the right to the tree of life and may go through the gates into the city. Outside are the dogs, those who practice magic arts, the sexually immoral, the murderers, the idolaters and everyone who loves and practices falsehood. I, Jesus, have sent my angel to give you this testimony for the churches. I am the Root and the Offspring of David, and the bright Morning Star. (Revelation 22:12–16, NIV)

> *If Jesus were to come today or send for you tonight, would you be ready?*

You are standing at the crossroads right now! Choose the good way that leads to Jesus. Be an overcomer! Won't you say "yes" to Jesus today? It does not matter what your past has been like. Whether you have lived a life of terrible sin or been a lukewarm Christian, you can choose life, blessing, and prosperity today—right now. Do not let your past dictate your future.

The Bible says you must be born again. When you are born again, old things pass away and all things become new. This is God's plan for your life. This is His way of restoring you. This is why you are alive.

Pray with me:

Dear Lord Jesus, I repent of my sins. Please forgive me for not giving You my all. This day as heaven and earth are my witness, I choose You. I choose life and blessings. This day I turn my back on those things in my life that are detestable to You. This day I vow to be obedient to You; I vow to follow Your commands and live for You. This day I vow to live a life holy and pleasing to You, the Great God above all gods. Dear Lord, give me the strength to be an overcomer so that how I live my life will be a witness to others. Thank You, Lord. Amen.

Date and sign below as your personal profession that you have chosen life this day!

I, _____, have chosen this day to serve the Lord God Almighty with all of my heart, mind, and soul. I choose this day blessings, life, and prosperity. I choose You, Jesus. This day, as I stand at the crossroads in my life, I choose the path that leads to heaven, the paradise of God. And if I should stumble or if I should fall—I will not give up. I will keep on seeking the Lord. I will not give up. I am an overcomer!

Date: _____

Congratulations! If you have done this, there is rejoicing going on in heaven over it: the Bible says that there is rejoicing in the presence of God's angels over just one sinner who repents (see Luke 15:7–10). Look at this day as the day you chose to change your life. Today, you drove a stake in the ground as your new starting point. There is a book referred to in the Bible as "the Book of Remembrance." I believe that as you make this commitment, this event is recorded in God's Book of Remembrance for all eternity (see Malachi 3:15–17).

Now that you have taken this step to live for Jesus, do not let anyone discourage you, not even the devil. People may try, Satan and his demons may try—but you are more than a conqueror.

At this time in your life, you may find that negative words begin to battle against you. Words are powerful, and they can affect us as we seek to live life beyond the crossroads—life in the service of Jesus. This is the subject of the next chapter, so read on!

Important Points
1. You too can have peace in Jesus with an eternal reward.
2. All that overcome shall experience God's blessings: here on earth, on Judgment Day, and in the paradise of God for all eternity.
3. Your walk with our Lord is a journey that will not end until you stand in His presence in the paradise of God.

Chapter 11

The Power of Words

WORDS ARE POWERFUl, and you'll need to understand their power as you try to live for Christ.

Has anyone ever spoken bad, negative words into your life? Do not listen to them or believe them.

Walt Disney, who founded Disneyland and became known throughout the world for his accomplishments, was fired from his newspaper job because they said he lacked creativity!

Beethoven, the world-famous composer, was referred to by his music teacher as a worthless composer!

Albert Einstein's school teacher told him he was mentally worthless!

Decca Records rejected the Beatles, saying that "guitar groups are on the way out."

If someone has spoken negative nonsense into your life, we rebuke it right now in the name of Jesus. *Lord God, we ask that You will remove all of the hurt of any mean, negative, undeserved words from any who read this and agree with me in prayer for You to do so.*

If what someone said about you is true and you want to change, you can start right now. This time, you're going to tap into the power of positive words—God's truth. I now speak the words of the God of All Creation, found in His holy scriptures, over you. Memorize these truths from the Holy Bible:

Jesus loves you.

You are more than a conqueror.

You shall be the head and not the tail.

He who trusts in the Lord shall prosper.

A good name is better than great riches.

God commands His angels concerning you.

You shall be the lender and not the borrower.

Blessed is the man who perseveres under trial.

God promises to never leave you nor forsake you.

The prayer of a righteous man is powerful and successful.

You can do all things through Christ Jesus who strengthens you.

Blessed are those whose names are found written in the book of life.

The angel of the Lord encamps around those who fear Him, and He delivers them.

God knows the plans He has for you: they are plans of hope and a future, plans to prosper you without harm.[5]

---

5. John 3:16, Romans 8:37, Deuteronomy 28:13, Psalm 1:3, Proverb 22:1, Psalm 91:11, Deuteronomy 15:6, James 1:12, Deuteronomy 31:6, James 5:16, Philippians 4:13, Revelation 3:5, Psalm 34:7, Jeremiah 29:11

There is great power in what we say. If your words about yourself are filled with doom and gloom, you are speaking doom and gloom over your life. However, if your words are positive and uplifting and speaking about where you want to be, then you are speaking life and success into your future. I love the scripture that says to speak things that are not as though they are (see Romans 4:17). This is simply speaking positively about your future.

When one of our daughters was a teenager and struggling with rebellion, my wife and I did a lot of this. We would just start speaking things out loud that we wanted for her. It felt good to do. At the time, she was far from the declarations we made, but we did it anyway. Today, she is not yet a preacher, teacher, or evangelist, but she is no longer the rebellious person she once was. She is married with two children and is a wonderful mother.

There is great power in the spoken word. In fact, it is written in Proverbs 18:21 that the tongue has the power of life and death. God created the heavens and the earth with the spoken word. You should be careful how you speak to and about people. We need to be quick to hear, slow to speak, and slow to anger.

What has your tongue been used for lately? In the last year, have you used your spoken words more to encourage, edify, and build up people, or have you used them more to hurt, discourage, and tear people down? Is this an area you need to work on?

When I grew closer to the Lord, the Holy Spirit convicted me because of my foul language, and I suspect He will do the same to you. It is a journey that will continue until you stand before the Lord in paradise. Go with it. When you hear your own words and they are harsh, discouraging, and hurtful, stop right there and apologize to the person you were speaking to. Believe me, after you do this a few times, it will help you to change your speech.

Even more difficult than controlling what you say and how you say it is the ability to keep your mouth shut when you really need to. There is a proverb that basically says that even a fool is thought wise when he keeps his mouth shut. Another says that if you can hold your tongue, you are wise. (See Proverbs 17:28 and Proverbs 13:3)

In the next two chapters, we're going to look at the most important words in the Christian life: the words of prayer.

Important Points

1. Has anyone spoken negative words into your life? Do not listen to them or believe them.

2. If what someone said about you is true and you want to change, you can start right now through the power of God's truth.

3. If your words are positive and uplifting and speaking about where you want to be, then you are speaking life and success into your future.

4. You should be careful how you speak to and about people. We need to be quick to hear, slow to speak, and slow to anger.

Chapter 12

Does God Really Answer Prayer?

HAVE YOU EVER ASKED YOURSELF if God really answers prayer? I know that not all of my prayers have been answered just as I asked. Looking back, I am thankful that many of them were not. My life would be much different from what it is today!

If you have been around other Christians for any length of time, I am sure you have heard them say, "You should pray about it," or "I will pray for you." We toss the idea of prayer around often. I wonder, though, how many people who say they will pray for you actually get around to doing it—and not just doing it, but praying that prayer that comes from the heart, that prayer that touches the heart of God. I do not claim to be an expert on prayer, but I can share my personal experiences on the matter.

Types of Prayer

One thing I have learned is that there are various levels and types of prayers that we all offer up to God. Let's take a look at them. Let's first look at the zero prayer. I call it a zero because that's what it is—a zero. I can best describe it with an example. My daughter had some friends over to watch the Super Bowl. One of the guys was definitely not a Steelers' fan. When they would get close to making a touchdown, he would say, "I rebuke that in Jesus' name." I think he was just joking, but then again, some people are really serious about their football!

When we toss prayer around jokingly, I call it a zero. Prayer is a serious matter and should not be taken lightly or done for show. Jesus said to watch out for people, even teachers and preachers, who speak prayers in public just for show. He said that such men will be severely punished (see Mark 12:40).

Next, let's look at what I call the fast-food prayer. These are the prayers you don't take the time to pray with sincerity. I have been guilty of this myself. Has anyone ever shared a desperate situation with you? A sick family member, a lost job, cancer, the death of a loved one—the list is endless. After someone shares a desperate situation with you, as many of us do, you casually state, "I will pray for you." When you leave that person, you say a quick five-second prayer, "Lord, please help that person," and you go about your business. I have done this out of obligation just because I had told someone "I will pray for you."

Fast-food prayers are offered out of obligation, and your heart is not in them. Instead, why not pray with the needy person right then? You don't have to create a public demonstration, but on the other hand, do not be ashamed of praying in public. You can take that person to the side, sit in the car, or, if it is a serious, desperate situation, take the time to meet in private and pray. Do not get me wrong: I am not saying not to offer up the quick, spontaneous prayer as you feel led. No, in fact just the opposite: you can and should give a quick prayer as you feel led in your heart. Whenever you pray, whether it's a long or a short prayer, do it with passion and faith. By faith, expect your prayers to be heard by the Lord God Almighty. If you tell someone you are going to pray for them, do it.

Desperate prayers are my favorite. This is when you cry out to God with all that you have. You have no one and nowhere else to turn. God is your only hope. In my opinion, these are the prayers that have a direct line to God the Father. The Bible has several historical examples of people calling out from their desperation and God hearing their prayers.

Even many non-Christians have heard of Jonah and the whale, found in the book of Jonah in the Holy Bible. Jonah was a prophet of God. God spoke to Jonah and told him to go to the mighty city of Nineveh. He was to tell them that their wicked ways had caught God's attention, and because of that He was going to bring destruction on them. Instead, Jonah boarded a ship and ran from the Lord. The Lord caused a violent storm to rise up, and the ship was about to sink. Jonah admitted that the storm was his fault for running from the Lord, so the crew threw him into the sea, and the sea became calm. The Lord caused a great fish to swallow Jonah, and he was inside the fish three days and three nights. The Bible states that he was in the belly of the fish with seaweed wrapped around his head.

The Bible says that from inside the fish, Jonah cried out to the Lord, and God heard his prayer. He, the God of All Creation, caused the great fish to vomit Jonah onto dry land. Now *that* is praying from a point of desperation! Can you imagine? Jonah was in the belly of a fish. The smell must have been terrible. Jonah had nowhere else to turn. Only God can help you in some situations!

There is something different about praying from a point of distress. It is like a direct line of communication to God the Father. Scripture reinforces that thought in many places.

> In my distress I called upon the LORD, and cried to my God: and he did hear my voice out of his temple, and my cry did enter into his ears. (2 Samuel 22:7, KJV)

> If calamity comes upon us, whether the sword of judgment, or plague or famine, we will stand in your presence before this temple that bears your Name and will cry out to you in our distress, and you will hear us and save us. (2 Chronicles 20:8, KJV)

> GOD answer you on the day you crash, the name God-of-Jacob put you out of harm's reach, send reinforcements from Holy Hill, dispatch from Zion fresh supplies, exclaim over your offerings, celebrate your sacrifices, give you what your heart desires, accomplish your plans. (Psalm 20:1–3, Message)

> But I will call on God, and the LORD will rescue me. Morning, noon, and night I cry out in my distress, and the LORD hears my voice. He ransoms me and keeps me safe from the battle waged against me, though many still oppose me. (Psalm 55:16–18, NLT)

Real-Life Miracles

Are miracles from God real? Decide for yourself. When I was around ten years old, my father was having severe chest pains. He suffered from high blood pressure, high cholesterol, and clogged arteries. It seemed like that year Dad was in the hospital more than he was at home. The doctors said that he needed open-heart surgery. They gave him a fifty-fifty chance to survive the operation, so Dad said, "Forget it." Without the surgery, the doctors thought he would live days, weeks maybe, a couple of months at most.

The thought of losing my dad at such a young age was more than I could bear, so I prayed. Every night I prayed myself to sleep. I cried out to God in my distress. I remember pleading with God not to take my dad until I was a grown man with a family of my own. I said, "God, I am just a young boy. I need my dad." My mother also prayed. She also called upon many others to join in with us, including the Oral Roberts Prayer Tower. (By the way, this prayer ministry is still in place. If you need prayer, you can call them at 918-495-7777.)

Well, I believe that the Lord God Almighty heard and answered our prayers. My dad lived another thirty-three years. Dad eventually had a heart bypass, but it was not until nearly twenty years later. He passed away at age seventy-four from other complications—it was not his heart that killed him. I believe with all my heart that Dad lived until I was an adult because of our prayers.

One summer when I was just sixteen years old, a friend of mine became a certified scuba diver and invited me to go diving at a huge lake not far from where we lived. We had heard there were some enormous fish down by the dam, so we made our own spears, picked up the scuba gear, and headed out. By this time in my life, I was already drinking every chance I got. We stopped and picked up some beer and headed out.

By the time we arrived at the lake, we'd already had a few beers. My friend told me that he had learned in scuba school that when you drink alcohol and scuba dive, it intensifies the effect. He said that a couple of beers could have the effect of a six-pack when under water; a six-pack could be more like a case—so being the adventurers we were, we decided to check it out. I had never scuba dived before, so I asked him for instructions, and he said, "Just follow me and watch what I do."

Well, as soon as we submerged I lost sight of my friend because the visibility was so poor. I swam around the dam looking for those large fish, and the next thing you know, I could not move. I was on the edge of passing out. I remember something mossy brushing up against my back, but it was so dark and the visibility so poor that I could not see what it was. I have no idea how deep I was. Thoughts of being sucked through the dam and spit out into the river below entered my mind.

In addition to the intensified alcohol effect on my body, I think I suffered from nitrogen narcosis, a condition that generally occurs at depths over one hundred feet. It can cause one to feel intoxicated to the point of passing out. As your depth increases, the effect of the narcosis increases, and you become more and more impaired. I remember watching the bubbles going up and thinking that if I could follow them, I would get to the surface—but I could not; I could not seem to move a muscle. To make matters worse, my regulator kept filling up with water, and I did not know how to clear it. I was drinking what seemed like gallons of water.

So I prayed. From my point of desperation, I prayed in my mind and asked for the Lord's help. I know it sounds a bit hypocritical to pray when you have been drinking. Nevertheless, I did. When you are at a point of desperation and there is absolutely no one else to help you, you pray with all your heart.

When I woke up, I was in an underwater cave—at least I thought I was. There were only a few inches of air space between the water surface and the top of the cave, just enough room for my face to be out of the water and breathing the air.

My mask was fogged over, and I could not see much at all. It was as if I was drifting in and out of consciousness.

I stayed there until the effects of the alcohol and the narcosis started to wear off. At this point, two or three hours had passed since I first started my dive, and my friend and the rangers were looking for me. The general opinion was that I had drowned. Voices filled my head, then noises. I started to wake up and realized that I was underneath a houseboat tied to the docks. The voices and noises were people above me. I went under again and came up between the docks and the houseboat. Some people saw me and pulled me up onto the dock, and I laid there for what seemed like hours as the effects continued to wear off. The search was off—I was found.

But here is the amazing part: I had been lost underwater for two or three hours, and my air tank only had approximately forty-five minutes of air supply. When they found me, I was all the way across the lake underneath the houseboat docks. This was a long way from where I had started—how did I get there? I know the answer! I cried out to God, and He answered my prayer.

Here is another personal example of God answering prayer. My family and I were on vacation on the Oregon coast. We decided to rent four-wheelers on the sand dunes near Coos Bay. It was a great day, and we had a blast. Chasing the waves and racing up and down the beach is an experience difficult to describe. It is just great fun. After a few hours, my wife and youngest daughter decided to take a break, so I took my two older daughters out to the big dunes. The rental yard warned us to be careful.

We raced out to the dunes and started having fun. My daughters are very adventurous. I looked over and saw Stephanie flying through the air. She was slightly raised up from her seat, arms bent, leaning forward, and my first thought was,

You go, girl. It looked like she had perfect form, flying through the air. That was until she crashed into a cliff wall head-on. She thrashed back and forth between the walls of the washout on the way to the bottom, and the four-wheeler landed on top of her, pushing her face into the sand. She lay there, apparently lifeless, face down in the sand.

I was climbing the dune next to hers and had a perfect view of the whole scene. I stopped and had to carefully back down the dune. I tried to pray, but only one word would come out of my mouth: the name "Jesus." The harder I tried to pray, the louder I repeated the name of Jesus. It was all I could say. *Jesus, Jesus, Jesus, Jesus*, all the way over to her. As I came closer to her, I saw what looked like her spirit coming back. It was as if the life came back into her. She picked her head up out of the sand, and it looked as if she had lost an eye from the goggles that were smashed on her face. I thought, *It is OK, because she is alive—thank you, Jesus!*

Stephanie could not move her legs. I picked her up, set her on my four-wheeler, and started back to the rental yard. I was praying for her all the way there. This is desperate prayer! In a situation like this, you have no one to turn to. All you have is prayer. Believe me, when something like that happens, you reach down inside of you, and you pray from the depths of your heart. There is no other thought or distraction to get in the way. It is just you at your point of desperation; you and your cry for mercy.

By the time we reached the rental yard some four to five miles away, Stephanie had regained some of the use of her legs. We set her in the backseat of the car and started for the hospital, praying every minute. Stephanie drifted in and out of consciousness all the way to the hospital. Lisa, my wife, held her, and she was also praying.

At the hospital, we discovered that her eye was OK. The goggles had cut a half-circle over the eye, and the flesh was covering it. There was blood in her ear, and the doctors said it was from a skull fracture. They took her in for a CAT scan, and we called everyone we knew to pray for her. The hospital staff brought her back, and another team of doctors came in to examine her again. They left and came back again with yet another examination.

We had been at the hospital for hours, and Stephanie seemed fine. She now had full movement in her legs, they had stitched up the wound above her eye, and she was being her silly self. Finally, when the doctors came in again, we asked for an explanation. They said that they did not understand. They knew there had been blood in her ear, on her eardrum, but now there was no trace of it. They said that with a skull fracture, blood on the eardrum is common. They anticipated her condition would get worse, that she would start slurring her words or talking and not making sense. One doctor said that the blood in the ear eventually dries up, but it takes a long time for it to come out. But Stephanie's ear now had no sign of it at all. We knew this was an answer to prayer.

The hospital wanted to keep her overnight, but Stephanie was up and around, so they discharged us and asked us to stay in town because they were still in disbelief. They said she might start to show the symptoms of a skull fracture later, and if she did, to rush her back to emergency. That night we rented a motel room, and Stephanie was fine. She even went swimming in the pool. This was, no doubt, a direct answer to prayer. It was a miracle. Today, years later, Stephanie is doing great. She just got back from a missions trip to Africa. Thank You, Jesus!

Do you pray? If not, please let me encourage you to do so. Prayer can change things. The Bible says to pray more about things and worry less. Why? Because prayer can change things, and worry can do nothing except make you sick in your body. That's right: the Bible says that worry and stress can shorten your life.

Do you get the picture yet? Well, there is more to prayer, so let's go on.

The Bible on Prayer

In the book of Job is found an intriguing scene. In my own words, it goes something like this: One day, the angels came before the Lord, and Satan came with them. The Lord said to Satan "Where have you been, Satan?" Satan, who roams around like a lion looking for people to destroy, answered, "I have been searching all over the earth." (1 Peter 5:8, KJV: "Be sober, be vigilant; because your adversary the devil, as a roaring lion, walketh about, seeking whom he may devour.")

The Lord God Almighty, knowing that Satan was looking for someone to harass, said, "Have you been to see my servant Job? What about him? Have you given him any thought?" Now, check this out. Satan himself answers in Job 1:9, "Does Job [reverently] fear God for nothing? Have you not put a hedge about him and his house and all that he has, on every side? You have conferred prosperity and happiness upon him in the work of his hands, and his possessions have increased in the land" (Amplified).

In the Contemporary English Version of the Bible, it says it like this: "'Why shouldn't he respect you?' Satan remarked. 'You are like a wall protecting not only him, but his entire family and all his property. You make him successful in whatever he does, and his flocks and herds are everywhere.'"

Satan is the first one to tell us that God has a hedge of protection around us. He admits that he can do nothing because of God's protection. In Bible days, people would plant a hedge around their property to keep people and animals out. Sometimes it was on a wall and had thorn bushes in it. When you pray, pray for a hedge of protection around you, your family, and your situation.

In these days, we live in a world that is filled with darkness, tragedy, and devastation. We urgently need the Lord's protection. The media is full of bad news, and it is as if the darkness is increasing. We need to incorporate prayer into our daily lives. First Thessalonians 5:17 says to pray constantly. You need to pray daily and often.

In these days we live in, we need God's hope and protection. One of the scriptures that encourages me is Psalm 91. I never get tired of it. I would encourage you to memorize it and repeat it often.

Psalm 91, CEV
THE LORD IS MY FORTRESS

Live under the protection of God Most High and stay in the shadow of God All-Powerful.
Then you will say to the LORD, "You are my fortress,
my place of safety; you are my God, and I trust you."
The Lord will keep you safe from secret traps and deadly diseases.
He will spread his wings over you and keep you secure.
His faithfulness is like a shield or a city wall. [Another definition for this verse is that he will protect you with a wall or shield.]
You won't need to worry about dangers at night or arrows during the day.
And you won't fear diseases that strike in the dark or sudden disaster at noon.
You will not be harmed, though thousands fall all around you.
And with your own eyes you will see the punishment of the wicked.
The LORD Most High is your fortress.

Run to him for safety, and no terrible disasters will strike
you or your home.
God will command his angels to protect you wherever you
go.
They will carry you in their arms, and you won't hurt your
feet on the stones.
You will overpower the strongest lions and the most deadly
snakes.
The Lord says, "If you love me and truly know who I am,
I will rescue you and keep you safe.
When you are in trouble, call out to me.
I will answer and be there to protect and honor you.
You will live a long life and see my saving power."

Important Points

1. When you pray, do it with sincere passion and faith. Expect
   your prayers to be heard by the Lord God Almighty.
2. At your point of desperation, when there is no one else to
   help you, pray with all of your heart.
3. Pray daily and often. Prayer can change things.
4. When you pray, pray a hedge of protection around yourself, your family, and your situation.

Chapter 13

Are Your Prayers Hindered?

IT WOULD BE WRONG FOR ME not to tell you about obstacles to prayer. Obviously, you cannot live an evil life with your back turned to God, with no regard to His ways, and expect His blessings and answers to your prayers without first turning to Him with a repentant heart, asking Him for forgiveness, and accepting Jesus Christ as your personal Savior. You must turn from your old ways, for the Bible tells us in 2 Timothy 2 to flee from the evil desires of our youth and strive for peace and righteousness, along with others who are doing the same.

To take it a step further, the Bible talks about specific conditions or sins that may hinder or cut our prayers off from being heard or answered. Let's take a look at a few of them.

Hindrances to Prayer

James 5 says that the prayer of a righteous person has great power. By contrast, an unrighteous person's prayer has

105

less power. There are none who are perfect or totally righteous; however, you need to strive toward righteousness. If you stumble or fall, do not give up. Pray and ask for forgiveness, and keep going!

> In the same way you married men should live considerately with [your wives], with an intelligent recognition [of the marriage relation], honoring the woman as [physically] the weaker, but [realizing that you] are joint heirs of the grace (God's unmerited favor) of life, in order that your prayers may not be hindered and cut off. [Otherwise you cannot pray effectively.] (1 Peter 3:7, Amplified Bible)

Let me put it this way: if you are violent and abusive to your spouse, it could hinder your prayers!

> And when ye spread forth your hands, I will hide mine eyes from you: yea, when ye make many prayers, I will not hear: your hands are full of blood. Wash you, make you clean; put away the evil of your doings from before mine eyes; cease to do evil; Learn to do well; seek judgment, relieve the oppressed, judge the fatherless, plead for the widow. Come now, and let us reason together, saith the Lord: though your sins be as scarlet, they shall be as white as snow; though they be red like crimson, they shall be as wool. If ye be willing and obedient, ye shall eat the good of the land. (Isaiah 1:15–20, KJV)

The fifty-eighth chapter of Isaiah expands the thought of Isaiah 1. I would encourage you to read it. It talks about how the

Israelite people fasted and prayed day after day; they even made frequent animal sacrifices. Day after day, they pursued God as if they were a people who did what was right in the sight of God and followed His commands. They asked God, "Why have we fasted and prayed and you do not answer our prayers? It is as if you do not even hear us." God answers them by saying, "Here is why: you go through the religious motions of fasting and praying, yet you still live a sinful, evil life. You cheat your workers, and your fasting ends with quarreling—fighting one another, striking others with your hands." God said, "You cannot live like this and expect your prayers to be heard."

> *The bottom line is that hypocritical religious*
> *activity is a hindrance to prayer.*

Unfortunately, this is a problem today. Don't let it be for you.

The Lord is far from the wicked, but He hears the prayer of the [consistently] righteous (the upright, in right standing with Him). (Proverbs 15:29, Amplified)

He who turns away his ear from hearing the law [of God and man], even his prayer is an abomination, hateful and revolting [to God]. (Proverbs 28:9, Amplified)

[Or] you do ask [God for them] and yet fail to receive, because you ask with wrong purpose and evil, selfish motives. Your intention is [when you get what you desire] to spend it in sensual pleasures. (James 4:3, Amplified)

If I regard iniquity in my heart, the Lord will not hear me. (Psalm 66:18, Amplified)

> We know that God does not listen to sinners;
> but if anyone is God-fearing and a worshiper of
> Him and does His will, He listens to him. (Psalm
> 66:18, Amplified)

That is worth repeating. If you are (1) God-fearing, (2) a worshiper of God, and (3) doing His will, then He, the God of all Creation, hears your prayer.

> No matter how much you pray, I won't listen. You are too violent. Wash yourselves clean! I am disgusted with your filthy deeds. *Stop doing wrong and learn to live right. See that justice is done. Defend widows and orphans and help those in need.* I, the LORD, invite you to come and talk it over. Your sins are scarlet red, but they will be whiter than snow or wool. If you willingly obey me, the best crops in the land will be yours.
> But if you turn against me, your enemies will kill you. I, the LORD, have spoken. (Isaiah 1:15–20, CEV, my emphasis)

Notice the crossroads here. God says that because you are too sinful and violent, He will not listen to your prayers, no matter how much you pray. *However, if you will stop doing wrong and learn to live right, He will bless you.* There are many crossroads mentioned in the Bible. Which direction will you take? One that leads to your prayers being answered, with your sins washed whiter than snow, or one that is against God's way?

How to Stop Hindering Your Prayers

We have been looking at many reasons your prayers might not be heard, but in Isaiah 1 the prophet gives us specific instructions on what we should be doing about it. They are found in verses 16 and 17. I already quoted them earlier.

1. Wash yourselves clean.
2. Stop doing wrong.
3. Learn to live right.
4. See that justice is done.
5. Defend widows and orphans.
6. Help those in need.
7. Obey the Lord.

When we add the instructions from the previous verses, we can place these in the list:

1. Be God-fearing.
2. Be a worshiper of God.
3. Willingly obey.

If a man did all these things, he would be the role-model Christian. Take these things to heart, for they all fall into the category of doing God's will! Other scriptures also talk about our prayers being hindered or ignored because of our sins. You can read them if you like. Here's a partial list: Micah 3:4, Deuteronomy 31:17–18, Deuteronomy 32:20, Psalm 13:1, Psalm 18:41, Isaiah 29:13, and Isaiah 59:2.

Isaiah sums this subject up by saying that some people honor God with their mouth, but their hearts are not in it. Don't be this way, for God is all-knowing, and He can see the deep, dark secrets in your heart. You cannot fool Him.

Be aware of these obstacles and adjust your life accordingly.

One of the basic principles of your prayers being heard and answered is that your life be in order. Walk in the power of God's Spirit and in obedience to the truth of His Word. Now, your life may be a wreck. You may be saying, "God will not hear me, nor will He answer." Not so! If you will U-TURN toward Him in your heart and mind, He will *help you* change your life!

> If my people, which are called by my name, shall humble themselves, and pray, and seek my face, and turn from their wicked ways; then will I hear from heaven, and will forgive their sin, and will heal their land. (2 Chronicles 7:14, KJV)

There are four steps in God's Directions for Our Restoration. Do you remember them?

God's Directions for Our Restoration

Humble yourself and pray.
Acknowledge your sins to the Lord in prayer.
Cry out to the Lord in repentance.

Seek His face.
Seek Him with all your heart, mind, and soul. Pray and read your Bible daily. Search for Him as you would a hidden treasure. Desire Him as an Olympic athlete desires the gold!

Turn from your wicked ways.
Turn from your sin. Make a U-TURN.
Resist the evil desires of your youth.
Remove those things in your life that are detestable to the Lord.
Do not conform any longer to the pattern of this world, but be transformed by the renewing of your mind.

Renew your covenant.
Renew your commitment to the Lord with all your heart and soul, and rejoice because of it. Write it down and tell a friend. Make it official.

No matter what your background, no matter what you have or have not done, you can turn to God. I love the scriptures that say, "The Lord is with you when you are with him!"

A Prayer of Victory

OK, so you have done it. You have asked God to forgive your sins, and you are seeking Him by reading your Holy Bible and praying. You have committed to turn from your wicked ways. You are not perfect, but you are honestly and sincerely striving to live a life in obedience to God's Word, not just hearing it but doing it. Congratulations! Your sins have been washed as white as snow (Isaiah 1:18, Psalm 51:7). What can stop you now? You know the things that can hinder your prayers: you have turned from them, you have humbled yourself and prayed for forgiveness, and you are seeking Him.

There's one more thing you should remember.

Satan your enemy wants to kill, steal, and destroy. Be aware that trials and tribulations will come your way. But as Jesus said, "Be of good cheer," because when your ways are right with the Lord, you can stand on His proven Word. Here is one to memorize:

> But in that coming day no weapon turned against you will succeed. You will silence every voice raised up to accuse you. These benefits are enjoyed by the servants of the LORD; their vindication will come from me. I, the LORD, have spoken! (Isaiah 54:17, NLT)

God's Word says that although trials and tribulations shall come your way, they shall not succeed. Know this, and when you find yourself in the middle of these trials and tribulations, stand firm. Put your trust in the Lord, and you will come through it.

Now it is time to pray a prayer of victory: Psalm 32. It is only eleven verses, and you really need to read it.

Psalm 32, NLT
A PSALM OF DAVID

Oh, what joy for those whose disobedience is forgiven, whose sin is put out of sight!

Yes, what joy for those whose record the LORD has cleared of guilt, whose lives are lived in complete honesty! When I refused to confess my sin, my body wasted away, and I groaned all day long. Day and night your hand of discipline was heavy on me. My strength evaporated like water in the summer heat. Finally, I confessed all my sins to you and stopped trying to hide my guilt. I said to myself, "I will confess my rebellion to the LORD." And you forgave me! All my guilt is gone. Therefore, let all the godly pray to you while there is still time, that they may not drown in the floodwaters of judgment. For you are my hiding place; you protect me from trouble.

You surround me with songs of victory. The LORD says, "I will guide you along the best pathway for your life. I will advise you and watch over you. Do not be like a senseless horse or mule that needs a bit and bridle to keep it under control." Many sorrows come to the wicked, but unfailing love surrounds those who trust the LORD. So rejoice in the LORD and be glad, all you who obey him! Shout for joy, all you whose hearts are pure!

Verse six says that everyone that is godly should pray. The Hebrew word for *godly* here is *hasid*. It is one of several Hebrew words for God's people, referring to them as people who are or should be devoted to God and faithful to him.

Prayer Do's (Not Don'ts!)

We have already covered many of the "don'ts" of prayer, so let's look now at what we should be doing. These are rules and guidelines drawn from scripture.

- Humble yourself and pray.
- Pray often.
- Let everyone who is godly pray.
- Pray for peace.
- Pray for those who persecute you.
- Pray for the sick.
- Pray for those who mistreat you.
- Pray that you will not fall into temptation.
- Pray in the Spirit on all occasions.
- Be joyful always and pray continually.
- Pray when you are in trouble.
- Pray for each other.
- Get on your knees and pray.
- Pray from your point of desperation.
- Fast and pray.
- Believe that you will receive what you ask for in prayer.
- Devote yourself to prayer.
- Do not be anxious about anything; rather present your requests to God.
- Lift up holy hands in prayer.
- Offer your prayers in faith.
- Pray on all occasions.
- Forgive others so that it will not be held against you when you pray.
- Strive to be holy and righteous so that your prayers may not be hindered.

- Pray a hedge of protection around yourself, your family, your friends, and situations in your life.
- Pray over your emotions, thoughts, finances, children, attitudes, and protection. [6]

When your ways are right with the Lord, you can confidently come before Him with your prayers. Jesus says, "Ask and it will be given to you; seek and you will find; knock and the door will be opened to you. For everyone who asks receives; he who seeks finds; and to him who knocks, the door will be opened" (Luke 11:9–10, NIV).

In my own words, the message of James 5:13–15 urges us, "Are you in trouble? You should pray. Are you sick? Call upon your Christian friends and leaders to pray over you and anoint you with oil in the name of Jesus. The prayer of faith will make the person better."

> Jesus told his disciples: Have faith in God! If you have faith in God and don't doubt, you can tell this mountain to get up and jump into the sea, and it will. Everything you ask for in prayer will be yours, if you only have faith. Whenever you stand up to pray, you must forgive what others have done to you. Then your Father in heaven will forgive your sins. (Mark 11:22–25, CEV)

Important Points

1. The Bible talks about specific actions or sins that will hinder or cut your prayers off from being heard or answered. Know what they are and stay away from them.

---

6. 2 Chronicles 7:14, Luke 5:16, Psalm 32:6, Jeremiah 29:7, Matthew 5:44, James 5:14, Luke 6:28, Luke 22:40, Ephesians 6:18, 1 Thessalonians 5:16–17, James 5:13, James 5:16, Daniel 6:10, Psalm 55:16–17, Ezra 8:23, Mark 11:24, Colossians 4:2, Philippians 4:6, 1 Timothy 2:8, James 5:15, Ephesians 6:18, Matthew 6:14–15, Psalm 66:18, Job 1:10

2. If you stumble or fall, do not give up. Pray and ask for forgiveness and keep going.

3. Jesus says, "Ask and it will be given to you; seek and you will find; knock and the door will be opened to you. For everyone who asks receives; he who seeks finds; and to him who knocks, the door will be opened."

Chapter 14

No Overdraft Protection

GOD IN HEAVEN ABOVE IS ALL KNOWING; He created the heavens and the earth and everything in them. He knows how many hairs are on top of your head. He even tells us in the Bible that He knew us before He formed us in the womb. I think it is safe to say that He even knows how long we will live. He knows exactly how many years, days, hours, and minutes are left to us.

So let's look at each life as a bank account. When we were born, God deposited X number of minutes into your account of life. Each and every day, you withdraw 1,440 minutes from your account. Your account is always going down, and only God knows your balance.

What did you spend your minutes on today? Did you spend them wisely or foolishly? Did you spend them helping or hurting people? Helping or hurting yourself? As you lay down to go to sleep at the end of each day, think about how you spent your minutes. You can never get minutes back; once they are gone, they are gone forever. There is no overdraft protection. Once your minutes are gone, your life is done here on earth, and you will enter into eternity either in heaven or in hell.

Think about your life so far. If others who know you were asked to describe you, what would they say? *She is a kind, loving person who is always helping others. He would give you the shirt off his back.* Or would they say that you are a drunken drug addict? *Watch out for that guy; he's trouble.* Whatever your background is, you can't change it. Don't live your life looking through the rearview mirror. You can, however, change your future. How do you want to be known? What is important to you? How should you be living your life?

Let me tell you about my Dad. He was raised in Chicago, Illinois, in a rough neighborhood and was sent off to military school at a young age. He joined the marines and served his time in Korea during the Korean War. He was in the heart of the bloody conflict, and this experience wounded him for life. After the military, he worked various jobs, but most involved working at a prison.

I do not remember Dad ever leading us in a prayer, even if it was just to bless our food during a meal. There was, however, a short season when Dad gave his heart to the Lord, and he was zealous for his faith. He started a Bible study and choir in the prison. This was short-lived, and he soon quit—I am not sure why. The rest of his life, he was known for being a hard man—so you can imagine our surprise when he made his comment on his deathbed.

He was in the hospital, and the doctors told us they didn't think he was going to make it through the night. My sister and I were there with him. We had sent Mom home because she had been at his side for days with hardly any rest. What do you say to your dad when this is likely the last time you will hear his voice? I said, "I love you, Dad." He said, "I love you guys too." He was weak, and it was as if he was fighting to speak any words at all.

I asked Dad if there was anything he wanted to say to us before he left us—any words of wisdom. He lay there for a moment, and then he said, with tears in his eyes, "Serve God and do His will, because nothing else matters."

Wow. Coming from my dad, that blew me away. Dad did make it through that night, but he never recovered. He passed away a short time later.

What does it mean to serve God and do His will? Why would a dying man say that nothing else matters? Dad's last words have driven me to take a look at the holy scriptures with new eyes, searching for what it means to "serve God and do His will." What I've found has inspired me to change my life's course once again. I now plan how I spend my minutes more carefully.

Let's take a look at just a few scriptures pointing us toward serving God and doing His will. Mark 12:29–31 gives the Greatest Commandment. A teacher of the law asked Jesus what the greatest commandment was. Jesus answered, "Love the Lord your God with all your heart and with all your soul and with all your mind and with all your strength. The second is this: Love your neighbor as yourself. There is no commandment greater than these" (NIV). This scripture tell us to love our neighbors as ourselves and God above all. In other words, it's not all about you! Show genuine concern for others through your actions, not just your words.

Isaiah 58:6–11 details the kinds of "religious activities" God wants to see from us:

> No, this is the kind of fasting I want: Free those
> who are wrongly imprisoned; lighten the burden
> of those who work for you. Let the oppressed go

free, and remove the chains that bind people. Share your food with the hungry, and give shelter to the homeless. Give clothes to those who need them, and do not hide from relatives who need your help. Then your salvation will come like the dawn, and your wounds will quickly heal. Your godliness will lead you forward, and the glory of the LORD will protect you from behind. Then when you call, the LORD will answer. "Yes, I am here," he will quickly reply. Remove the heavy yoke of oppression. Stop pointing your finger and spreading vicious rumors! Feed the hungry, and help those in trouble. Then your light will shine out from the darkness, and the darkness around you will be as bright as noon. The LORD will guide you continually, giving you water when you are dry and restoring your strength. You will be like a well-watered garden, like an ever-flowing spring. (NLT)

Do we become so occupied with "the Lord's work" that we lose sight of the precious *people* God has called us to serve? Do we become so preoccupied with our mission and our gifts that we neglect a charitable attitude toward our families and other people around us? Look at how God says to serve Him:

- Love your neighbor as yourself.
- Stick up for prisoners unjustly chained.
- Help the abused.
- Feed the hungry.
- Help the poor and homeless.
- Give clothes to those in need.
- Help your relatives in need.
- Don't mistreat others or falsely accuse them.

When you really grasp these scriptures and take them to heart, the fruits you bear will be pleasing to your God. For if you love your God, you will seek Him; you will pursue Him with passion. If you seek Him with true-hearted loyalty, you will find Him. And if you do this, the Holy Spirit will begin to fill you and flow through you.

Choosing the Right Church

If you want to live a life of service to God, you will need to be around other Christians. Find a Bible-based, Jesus-believing church, and go every time the doors are open. Bring a notepad and take notes. Ask questions when you do not understand.

What church should you go to? Good question. Today, there are so many to choose from. To make things worse, many of churches claim they are the one. Some claim they are *the* only one! But here is the most important factor: Does the church you are considering believe that Jesus is the only Son of God? That He was born of a virgin, lived a sinless life, was crucified for our sins, rose from the dead on the third day, and was exalted to the right hand of God?

There are many false religions out there today. They were prophesied about thousands of years ago. First Timothy 4:1–2 warns, "The Spirit clearly says that in later times some will abandon the faith and follow deceiving spirits and things taught by demons. Such teachings come through hypocritical liars, whose consciences have been seared as with a hot iron" (NIV).

First John 4:1–3 says, "Dear friends, do not believe every spirit, but test the spirits to see whether they are from God, because many false prophets have gone out into the world. This is how you can recognize the Spirit of God: Every spirit that acknowledges that Jesus Christ has come in the flesh is from God, but every spirit that does not acknowledge Jesus is not from God. This is the spirit of the antichrist, which you have heard is coming and even now is already in the world" (NIV).

If a church does not believe that Jesus is the only begotten Son of God, that He was born by a virgin birth, that He died for our sins when He was crucified on the cross, and that He rose on the third day and now sits at the right hand of God the Father, then they are one of the false, deceiving churches prophesied about. Run from them: they will try to suck you into their deception.

The Holy Bible was written thousands of years ago and has survived the test of time. It is the only book that has had dozens of prophecies come to pass. It warns us not to add or take away from its writings. Revelation 22:19 proclaims, "And if anyone takes words away from this book of prophecy, God will take away from him his share in the tree of life and in the holy city, which are described in this book" (NIV). If a church has written its own Bible, scriptures, or holy writings, I would not associate with it. The Holy Bible must be the center of their beliefs and teachings; without this they are in deception.

Important Points
1. Do not live your life looking through the rearview mirror. You can influence and direct your future.
2. Your life is not just about you. Your life will impact the people around you; therefore heed the words of Jesus and show genuine concern for others through your actions, not just your words. Love your neighbor as yourself.
3. If you want to live a life of service to God, you will need to be around other Christians.
4. If a church has written its own Bible, scriptures, or holy writings, I would not associate with it. The Holy Bible must be the center of their beliefs and teachings; without this they are in deception.

Chapter 15

When Faced With a Mountain

WE ARE ALL FACED WITH UPS AND DOWNS in our lives. It does not matter who you are, how wealthy or poor you may be, your race or gender or position in life. Life's trials and tribulations will hit each and every one of us at some point. So what can get you through in your time of need?

I think of life as a range of peaks and valleys. The mountaintop experiences are the good times, when you seem to be on top of the world, when everything is going well for you. The valleys are just the opposite. These are the times when you feel down and out.

Life is easy when you are in a season of mountaintop experiences, but when you are in the valley, it is tough to keep going. Look back on your life, and I am sure you will relate. Ask yourself a question, though, when you think about the valleys. What did you learn in them? Personally, I think I have learned more during my valley experiences than during my seasons on top of the mountain.

When I was a boy, my mother enjoyed a Christian television program called *The Hour of Power* by Dr. Robert H. Schuller. This guy always had a smile on his face and seemed full of peace. He was very inspirational and always closed his program with a positive thought, leaving a good feeling in your heart. He came up with what he called "The Possibility Thinker's Creed."

Schuller made a medallion with a shepherd taking care of his sheep on the front (symbolizing Jesus taking care of us) and that inspirational creed on the back. I have carried it around in my pocket for over thirty years. Interestingly enough, I faithfully carry it when I am in a valley season in my life—not so much when I am on the mountaintop, unless I am pushing on toward accomplishing a vision or major goal in my life. I carry it because it is a reminder that I will not quit, and that with God's help, I am more than a conqueror. When I walk, I hear it jingling with my keys or the change in my pocket, and the sound reminds me to persevere. When I get home after a long day and empty my pockets, it is there: a reminder not to give up.

If you are like most of us, you tend to depend on God more when you're aware of need in your life than when you're not. When you have money in the bank and can have whatever you want for dinner or go out to eat anytime you want, you tend not to lean on God for provision as you would if your shelves, refrigerator, and bank account were empty. So whatever your situation in life, rich or poor, in good health or sickness, you need to learn to lean on and trust in God at all times. He alone is our strength and our refuge. In Him alone should we put our trust.

Do You Need to Repent?

An example of a mountain you may be facing is this: Some of you have hungry children but choose to buy alcohol or drugs instead of food for your kids. If that's you, I also believe that this rips you up inside, because you're letting your addictions take priority over food for the kids. Please listen to me now. You can overcome this mountain with God's help. Isaiah 45:2 says, "I will go before you and will level the mountains, I will break down gates of bronze and cut through bars of iron" (NIV). In order to have this faith and trust in God, you must be in right standing with Him! You have to go through the process of repentance, and then you can count on God to intervene on your behalf. He even says He will command His angels concerning you!

Remember Psalm 91 from chapter 12? It tells us that *if* we seek refuge in the Lord our God through faith and trust in Him, *then* He will command His angels concerning us so that no disaster or harm shall fall upon us.

It boils down to this: accept Jesus as your personal Savior and seek Him with all your heart, learning to do His will, and the God of All Creation will bless you, guide you, and protect you. When you read God's Word about His blessings and protection, you can do so with confidence and know that His Word applies to you. Understand that no one is perfect, and there is no human who will become perfect from this point on. No, you will still have ups and downs. You may even mess up from time to time, but when and if you do, you can ask Jesus to forgive you and help you to overcome. It is a matter of the heart. If you are truly striving to live a Christian life, God knows it.

Check this out: My sister gave me a Bible that was printed in 1787. It has "Practical Observations" written throughout, and it says this about Psalm 91: "We may see in this psalm how happy those are that trust in God, and draw near to him. God commands his angels to keep them from all dangers; he loves them tenderly; he preserves them from every thing that might hurt them, delivers them when they call upon him in their distress, and heaps upon them all kinds of blessings. These glorious privileges and excellent promises are very proper to comfort and encourage all such as fear God, and to fill them with unspeakable joy and unshaken confidence."[7]

> *You really can live this new life,*
> *both on the mountains and in the valleys.*

If you have not yet done this, get on your knees before the God of All Creation and ask for forgiveness. Ask Him to help you out of this lifestyle. Ask Him to direct your paths and give you the strength to be an overcomer. Go right now to someone who can help you—a Christian friend or family member or your local Christian church—and tell them you are ready for change. Tell them that you got on your knees and repented and asked God to help you change your life. Ask them to help you find a mentor who will help you stay sober and keep you accountable.

Once you do this, you need to learn to trust in God. You need this constant reminder that God is with you and will help you if you turn to Him. One great way to keep this reminder in front of you is to read the words on a penny every time a penny comes before you. You will find the words "In God We Trust" inscribed on it. Every time a penny touches your hand, take a few seconds to read this and say a silent prayer: *Thank You, Lord God, that my trust is in You and not in man. Thank You for taking care of me.* Try this: it can be a powerful reminder to trust in Him.

Overcoming Fear

There is one more topic to address before we finish this talk of mountains and valleys. Do you suffer from fear? Don't be ashamed to admit it: you are not alone. Even so, you must understand that ungodly fear is not of God. It is of the enemy.

---

7. Rev. J.F. Ostervald, "Practical Observations" in The Holy Bible. Newcastle-Upon-Tyne: M. Brown, 1787.

"For God did not give us a spirit of fear; but of power, and of love, and of a sound mind" (2 Timothy 1:7, KJV). Unnecessary, unhealthy fear is a tool that our enemy the devil tries to use against us. But knowing this can help us overcome fear: you see, *the devil is a liar*. He is the king of deception. When you hear a bad report from people, do not focus on it. Focus on the report of God and His promises. You can do it! Never give up. Learn to trust and lean on God.

As you trust in God, you can learn to fight fear with fear. The Bible tells us to "Serve only the Lord your God and fear him alone" (Deuteronomy 13:4, NLT) and that "Fear of the Lord is the beginning of wisdom" (Proverbs 9:10, KJV). The Hebrew word for fear, *yir`ah*, signifies awe in regard to what is unknown. Mostly it means *reverence*, particularly for God. This does not imply that we need to be afraid of God, but it does require the appropriate recognition and respect for God's fearsome qualities, such as His righteous wrath. The fear of God—that is, the proper respect for God—compels us to abandon our evil ways and teaches us wisdom. Fear of God leads to confidence in this life, for if we have submitted to the Almighty, we do not have to fear any other power in this world. The Almighty Creator of the Universe is our protector.

Important Points
1. You need never quit, because you are more than a conqueror with God's help.
2. You can overcome any mountain with God's help.
3. Fear of God leads to confidence in this life, for if we have submitted to the Almighty, we do not have to fear any other power in this world.

Chapter 16

Forgiveness

THIS IS A VERY IMPORTANT TOPIC, and if you want to follow God, you've got to learn it. Some of you are holding onto things that happened to you as a child and have plagued you all of your life. I will not for one minute make light of whatever happened to you. I have heard the terrible stories and observed some things firsthand. But forgiveness is necessary for your growth as a person and an overcomer.

Years of holding onto these hurts make them difficult to shed. When I was a young boy, my dad planted a willow tree in our backyard. He drove a metal stake in the ground and made his own rope sling with a piece of old garden hose to keep the rope from cutting into the bark. This tree grew as I did, and I soon left Mom and Dad's house—Dad kicked me out, as I wrote about earlier. Maybe ten years after I left home, my wife and I bought the house from my parents, and we moved in. That tree was still there, as was the metal stake. The metal stake was almost four feet tall, but all that was now showing was about three inches. The tree had grown up and around the metal post, almost completely encasing it. We sold that house nearly ten years ago, so by now, I am sure you cannot see the post at all.

How does this relate to unforgiveness, you ask? Well, it is very similar. At first, you can remove the stake without any damage to the tree. The longer you wait to remove it, the more removing it will damage the tree. Today, you could not remove that stake without killing the tree. When you hold on to unforgiveness for many years, it becomes impossible to remove it from your life totally and completely without God's help. But nothing is impossible with God. To get long-held unforgiveness out of your life, you need to know God's Word on this subject.

First of all, we need to understand that God's holy written Word tells us that we need to forgive those who have sinned against us in order for God to forgive us of our sins.

> For if ye forgive men their trespasses, your heavenly Father will also forgive you: But if ye forgive not men their trespasses, neither will your Father forgive your trespasses. (Matthew 6:14–15, KJV)

I know this may be difficult for many of you, but it needs to be done. The types of child abuse I hear about most frequently are sexual, physical, verbal, and mental abuse. Many people have suffered these types of abuse, including my wife. She talks about when her mother shoved her through a Sheetrock wall. Her childhood experiences have bothered her for many years, but Lisa has been encouraged to put those experiences behind her, and now she helps others by telling the testimony of her childhood and how she had to work through forgiveness.

Lisa will tell you that one of her favorite resources to lean on is Joyce Meyers Ministries. I think it was over twenty years ago when Joyce Meyers came to our church and spoke about how she was sexually abused as a young girl. She told us of the abuse she suffered and how she held onto it for years. If I remember right, she also told us that it was not until she totally and completely forgave her father that her ministry exploded.[8] When I hear about forgiveness from someone who has been there and done that, it carries more power for me than if I was to hear about it from someone who hasn't experienced the abuse and forgiveness but may have some book knowledge. Maybe it's the same for you.

Joyce has two books on forgiveness that you must read if you struggle with forgiveness. The first is *The Power of Forgiveness*, and the second is *Forgive and Live Again*. The titles alone have truths in them! Unforgiveness can hinder your prayers, thus holding you back. You also need to forgive *yourself*. Yes, many of us have done mean, maybe even terrible, things to others, and you may be holding onto those things. You need to work through it, let it go, forgive yourself, and get on with your life. If you can, make things right with the person you have hurt. This might just mean saying you are sorry and asking for forgiveness. Whatever it was, pray about making it right, but make sure you do not bring any harm to yourself or others in the process. There may not be any physical way to make things right, and if that's the case, you may just have to ask for God's

8. Joyce Meyers is one of my favorite preachers and teachers. She has a gift of telling like it is. It doesn't matter what walk of life you come from: her ability to communicate Bible truths and teach the Word of God in a way you can relate to and apply in your daily life is second to none. Back when we heard her, she did not have dozens of books, tapes, and teachings as she does now. You will have to read her books or hear her testimony on TV to get the whole story, and I encourage you to do just that.

forgiveness and then forgive yourself. Once you do this, you can begin to live again. One thing you must understand is that God forgives you no matter what!

When I was maybe ten years old, I was riding my bike down the sidewalk, and a kid who lived around the corner was walking toward me. We didn't get along with these kids—I'm not sure why. They were the new kids who had moved in with the new subdivisions. I think we disliked them because their new houses took the fields that we had enjoyed playing in. We would have rock fights on a regular basis. Thank God no one was ever seriously hurt!

On this particular occasion, I was riding my bike down the sidewalk, and here came one of these boys—so I spit on him as I rode by. It hit him right in the face. Looking back, I realize I was a punk for doing this.

I really didn't think about it again until some twenty-seven years later when I was tying down our truck with a last load of furniture. I was only minutes away from leaving California as we were moving to Idaho. For some reason, this event was weighing heavily on my heart. It was like having a conversation with the Lord about it. I was deeply convicted and wondered if my action had bothered that boy—now a man—throughout the years. I felt like the Lord was prompting me to find him and ask his forgiveness. I said, "Lord, that was years ago, and I haven't seen him in years. I wouldn't know where to begin to look for him."

As I walked out to the truck to get ready to leave, much to my amazement, here came that same man walking down the street! He was mostly bald now, but I knew exactly who he was. My heart rate jumped, I started to sweat, and I said, "You have got to be kidding, Lord."

The man was walking down the middle of the street instead of on the sidewalk, as if he was keeping his distance from a once-known jerk. I wrestled back and forth in my spirit. Was I going to say anything, or was I going to hide? Finally, I walked out to the middle of the street and confronted him. I asked if he remembered me, and he said he did. I told him that I was a Christian now and that the Lord had convicted me for being so mean to him as a kid. He said he didn't remember that, so I reminded him of the incident that was bothering me. I said I was sorry and asked him for his forgiveness. It was a difficult thing for me to do—I almost cried! He told me not to worry about it and that he too was a Christian. He had moved away and was just visiting his parents, who still lived in the neighborhood. When he left, I still felt bad for any pain and suffering I might have caused that boy, yet at the same time I felt a release because I had confronted him and asked for forgiveness.

There are many Bible stories about people who did wrong things and God forgave them when they cried out to God in repentance. Have you heard what David did as king? He saw a beautiful woman and asked, "Who is that?" They said it was Bathsheba, wife of Uriah the Hittite, a soldier who was off to war. Knowing she was a married woman, David took advantage of his rights as king and sent for her. He slept with her, and she became pregnant. To cover up his mistake, he had her husband brought back from the battlefront. When Uriah arrived, King David asked him for an update on how the war was going. Then he got Uriah drunk and said to himself, *Now he'll go home and sleep with his wife, and no one will ever know what I did.*

In the morning, David discovered that Uriah had slept on the floor in the palace with the servants. When David asked him why he hadn't gone home, Uriah said, "All the other men are out to war where I should be; therefore, I shall not go home until they all go home." So King David sent Uriah back to war with a sealed message for the leader of the army. It said, "Put Uriah in the front lines at the source of the heaviest fighting and then withdraw from him and leave him there." They did this, and Uriah died. David took Bathsheba as his wife and thought he'd gotten away with it all. But God saw it all—you cannot fool God!

After this, God then sent his prophet Nathan to David, saying, "God has seen your sinful acts, and the son born to you and Bathsheba shall die." David cried out in repentance and asked for forgiveness, and God did forgive him—but his new son did in fact die. After David experienced all of this, he wrote Psalm 51. Read it a few times over and think about what it says.

> Have mercy upon me, O God, according to thy loving kindness: according unto the multitude of thy tender mercies blot out my transgressions. Wash me throughly from mine iniquity, and cleanse me from my sin. For I acknowledge my transgressions: and my sin is ever before me.
>
> Against thee, thee only, have I sinned, and done this evil in thy sight: that thou mightest be justified when thou speakest, and be clear when thou judgest. Behold, I was shapen in iniquity; and in sin did my mother conceive me. Behold, thou desirest truth in the inward parts: and in the hidden part thou shalt make me to know wisdom. Purge me with hyssop, and I shall be clean: wash me, and I shall be whiter than snow. Make me to hear joy and gladness; that the bones which thou hast broken may rejoice. Hide thy face from my sins, and blot out all mine iniquities. *Create in me a clean heart, O God; and renew a right spirit within me. Cast me not away from thy presence; and take not thy holy spirit from me. Restore unto me the joy of thy salvation; and uphold me with thy free spirit.*

Then will I teach transgressors thy ways; and sinners shall be converted unto thee.

Deliver me from bloodguiltiness, O God, thou God of my salvation: and my tongue shall sing aloud of thy righteousness. O Lord, open thou my lips; and my mouth shall shew forth thy praise. For thou desirest not sacrifice; else would I give it: thou delightest not in burnt offering. The sacrifices of God are a broken spirit: a broken and a contrite heart, O God, thou wilt not despise. Do good in thy good pleasure unto Zion: build thou the walls of Jerusalem. Then shalt thou be pleased with the sacrifices of righteousness, with burnt offering and whole burnt offering: then shall they offer bullocks upon thine altar. (Psalm 51, KJV, my emphasis)

The verses italicized above are often sung. They make a beautiful song that will touch the innermost part of your heart and soul.

Important Points

1. One thing you must understand is that God forgives you no matter what you have done! However, you must forgive others who have sinned against you so that your Heavenly Father can forgive you.

Chapter 17

From the Pit to the Palace in One Day

AS WE CLOSE THIS BOOK, I wanted to leave you with a powerful thought: your circumstances can change very quickly when God is on your side.

It does not always happen like this, but with God all things are possible for those who trust in Him. This theme that all things are possible with God's help is found in various locations throughout the Bible, including Matthew 19:26, Mark 9:23, and Mark 10:27.

Let me tell you about Joseph. He was one of twelve brothers born to Jacob. Jacob loved Joseph more than the others and spoiled him rotten; he even had a beautiful coat of many colors made for Joseph and nothing for the eleven others. The brothers were jealous and despised Joseph, and one day they seized him and sold him into slavery. They told Jacob that Joseph had been eaten by a wild animal.

As a slave, Joseph found himself working in a palace in Egypt, and the boss's wife wanted to sleep with him, but Joseph refused. She became angry with him and had him thrown into prison, telling all that he had attempted to rape her. Joseph was now a foreigner in an Egyptian prison. He was there for several years, when one day, Pharaoh, the leader of Egypt, had Joseph brought to him. Pharaoh had heard that Joseph was able to interpret dreams through the God he served.

Joseph did in fact interpret Pharaoh's dream with God's help, and he was promoted from prisoner to second-in-command in all of Egypt, outranked only by Pharaoh himself. This is the equivalent of having an illegal alien in the USA in prison for attempted rape, and in one day he goes from behind the prison bars to the office of vice president of the United States. This is what the God we serve can do.[9]

The God we serve is omnipotent, all-powerful. He is the God who created all things. He parted the sea, He stopped time, He is the God who answers prayer. He knows how many hairs are on top of your head, He knows how many stars are in the sky, and He cares for you. If you have not done so yet, won't you give your life and eternity over to Him? He is waiting for you with open arms!

You can change your life if you want to. Those of you who are ready and willing and will give it your best effort now: I salute you. I will be praying for you. Remember this: If you stumble and if you fall, never, never give up! Get up off the ground, brush yourself off, and keep going. *You can do this*, and there are great things in store for you. You are more than a conqueror—I believe in you!

---

9. There is much more to this story, and it is awesome! You can read it in Genesis chapters 37–50.

Part 4

Tools for Your New Life

At-Risk Quiz

How do you know if you are at risk? Take this short quiz:

Has your partying caused you any harm? Physically,
emotionally or financially?
    ___Yes ___No

Has your partying caused any harm to others?
    ___Yes ___No

Do you struggle to quit using drugs and/or alcohol?
    ___Yes___ No

Do you think your life is headed for trouble?
    ___Yes___ No

If you answered yes to any of the questions above, you may
be at risk and in need of help.

Simple Steps to Overcoming

- Pray, every day, often.
- Never give up. You can do this!
- Find Christian friends and spend time with them.
- Find a Bible-based, Jesus-believing church and go every time the doors are open.
- Change your environment so that you are no longer around temptations.
- Most importantly, *read your Holy Bible daily*. I suggest you read the Gospel of John first. Then read the entire New Testament, starting in Matthew. Once you finish the New Testament, start in Genesis and read the entire Old Testament.

Stand at the crossroads and look;
ask for the ancient paths,
ask where the good way is,
and walk in it,
and you will find rest for your souls.

JEREMIAH 6:16, NIV

**IF YOU SEEK HIM,
THEN YOU WILL FIND HIM.**
Jeremiah 29:13-14; Deuteronomy 4:29; Proverbs 8:17;
Proverbs 11:27; Matthew 7:7-8; Luke 11:9-10; Acts 17:27

Seek the Lord, and a year from now
your life will be very different than it is today.

You decide. The choice is yours.
Blessings or Curses?
It is the choice of a lifetime.
Which way will you go?

The Ten Commandments
From Exodus 20:3–17, NIV

1. You shall have no other gods before me.
2. You shall not make for yourself an idol in the form of anything in heaven above or on the earth beneath or in the waters below.
3. You shall not misuse the name of the Lord your God, for the Lord will not hold anyone guiltless who misuses his name.
4. Observe the Sabbath day by keeping it holy.
5. Honor your father and mother.
6. You shall not murder.
7. You shall not commit adultery.
8. You shall not steal.
9. You shall not lie.
10. You shall not covet.

God's Directions for Our Restoration

Humble yourself and pray.

> Acknowledge your sins to the Lord in prayer.
> Cry out to the Lord in repentance.

Seek His face.

> Seek Him with all your heart, mind, and soul. Pray and read your Bible daily. Search for Him as you would a hidden treasure. Desire Him as an Olympic athlete desires the gold!

Turn from your wicked ways.

> Turn from your sin. Make a U-turn.
> Resist the evil desires of your youth.
> Remove those things in your life that are detestable to the Lord.
> Do not conform any longer to the pattern of this world, but be transformed by the renewing of your mind.

Renew your covenant.

> Renew your commitment to the Lord with all your heart and soul, and rejoice because of it. Write it down and tell a friend. Make it official.

If Jesus Were to Come Today or Send for You Tonight, Would You Be Ready?

You are standing at the crossroads right now! Choose the good way that leads to Jesus. Be an overcomer! Won't you say "yes" to Jesus today? It does not matter what your past has been like. Whether you have lived a life of terrible sin or been a lukewarm Christian, you can choose life, blessing, and prosperity today, right now. Do not let your past dictate your future.

The Bible says you must be born again. When you are born again, old things pass away and all things become new.

Pray with me:

Dear Lord Jesus, I repent of my sins. Please forgive me for not giving You my all. This day as heaven and earth are my witness, I choose You. I choose life and blessings. This day I turn my back on those things in my life that are detestable to You. This day I vow to be obedient to You; I vow to follow Your commands and live for You. This day I vow to live a life holy and pleasing to You, the Great God above all gods. Dear Lord, give me the strength to be an overcomer so that how I live my life will be a witness to others. Thank You, Lord. Amen.

Date and sign below as your personal profession that you have chosen life this day!

I,_____, have chosen this day to serve the Lord God Almighty with all of my heart, mind, and soul. I choose this day blessings, life, and prosperity. I choose You, Jesus. This day, as I stand at the crossroads in my life, I choose the path that leads to heaven, the paradise of God. And if I should stumble or if I should fall—I will not give up. I will keep on seeking the Lord. I will not give up. I am an overcomer!

Date: _____

The Thirty-Day Challenge: What It Is, How to Do It

What Is the Thirty-Day Challenge?

The Thirty-Day Challenge is a personal pledge of total commitment to begin the process of change in your life with God's help in passionate pursuit of Him with all your heart through prayer, study of the Holy Bible, worship in song, and fellowship with other Christians for thirty days.

How to Do the Thirty-Day Challenge

To complete the Thirty-Day Challenge successfully, you have to plan for it. First and foremost, you have to make the time. Schedule it! It must take priority over TV, the Internet, hobbies, sports, and anything else that distracts you. The more you put into it, the more you will get out of it. This is no half-hearted effort! If you are not willing to give the challenge your best effort, you may not want change badly enough. If you are desperate for change, you will go for it.

1. Get a small calendar book and schedule your day. Schedule your time with God. You will need to spend more time in pursuit of your relationship with God than ever before in your life.
2. Give it all you can for thirty days. The more you put into it, the more you will get out of it. Target spending at least one hour per day praying and reading your Bible. Keep a logbook and write notes, recording what the Lord is speaking to you through your prayers and study of His Word, the Holy Bible.
3. Make it a priority. You can count on life's distractions to come your way, so plan on saying "no." During these thirty days, you have to be able to tell people that you are in-

volved in the process of change in your life. It is a priority, and your schedule is full right now.

4. Find a Jesus-preaching, full-Bible Christian church that loves to worship God with live music, and go every time the doors are open. Go to all the functions. Be bold in meeting Christians: they will help you on your journey. Be open and honest.

5. Set up reminders in places you frequent every day. A post-it on your bathroom mirror saying "I CAN DO THIS" or a note on your workspace that says "THIRTY-DAY CHALLENGE" can help keep you on track. I like to post scriptures that say "I am more than a conqueror with God's help" or "I can do all things through Christ Jesus who strengthens me."

6. Carry a reminder for the entire thirty days. I have a medallion with a special motivational message on it. What can you carry as a reminder? Try finding a penny made the year you were born. Carry it always. Every time you see it, read the inscription: "In God We Trust." When you are faced with temptation or a difficult time, hold it in your hand and pray for God's strength. If you are in public, you can pray silently in your head. The idea is to set your heart and thoughts on the God of All Creation in all areas of your life during these thirty days.

I challenge you to do this faithfully for just thirty days. If you do so with sincere intentions of drawing closer to your Lord and Savior Jesus, I guarantee you will. The Bible says in Jeremiah 29:13 , "'When you seek me with your whole heart I will be found by you and I will restore you' declares the Lord" (NIV). This could be the beginning of your new life.

To Make an Action Plan, You Will:

- Write down a specific goal you want to accomplish.

- Identify all the steps to accomplish that goal.

- Prioritize each step.

- Calendarize the steps, with due dates for each one.

- Publish your Action Plan: do not keep it a secret.

- Select a sponsor or accountability partner and share your Action Plan.

- Decide on frequency to meet with your sponsor.

- Decide on any accountability guidelines.

Instructions for Creating Your Action Plan

1. Develop your goal statement, and be specific.

You are not trying to impress anyone with a fancy statement that can be posted on a wall. Unfortunately, this is what happens to most so-called "Vision Statements"—they get posted somewhere, and in actuality they mean nothing. Not yours. Your goal statement is not only what you want to accomplish, but what you desperately need to do to change your life. Don't get caught up in the game of "Will others be impressed with it?" No, you must ask yourself, what does this mean to me?

Here are some examples of a goal statement:

- I will beat the drug and alcohol addiction in my life, make new sober friends, and become a successful, healthy, prosperous person with God's help.
- My life will do a U-TURN away from my destructive habits and addictions. I will become blessed and highly favored. With God's help I will restore my family and become a helper to those who have struggled with the same issues.

2. Identify the necessary steps to accomplish your goal.

Think about this carefully, and write down your ideas. Be honest, for you are trying to change your life, not impress anyone. Everyone's situation is different, but your list might look something like this:

- Stay away from people who drag me down.
- Stay away from the partyers in my life.
- Change my phone number.
- Move.
- Get professional help.
- Join a Christian support group like Celebrate Recovery.
- Start going to a Christian church.

- Find Christian friends to hang out with.
- Find a sponsor or accountability partner.
- Read every scripture in the Bible that speaks about drugs and alcohol.

Depending on how bad your situation is, you may need to do spiritual surgery. For example, if you have roommates and there are drugs and alcohol in your house every day, you need to move to get away from it. Sometimes others can suggest things you need to do. I remember my parents and others telling me not to hang around those crazy friends of mine. They said, "You will only get in trouble, and they will drag you down." They were right. A probation officer once told me that my alcohol usage was causing me problems and that was why I was in his office. My first step in turning from the trouble was to accept the fact that alcohol was causing me problems.

3. Prioritize your list.

To do this, simply put the list in order from one to however many steps there are. Start with first things first.

- Stay away from people who drag me down.
- Stay away from the partyers in my life.
- Read every scripture in the Bible that speaks about drugs and alcohol.
- Join a Christian support group like Celebrate Recovery.
- Start going to a Christian church.
- Find Christian friends to hang out with.
- Find a sponsor or accountability partner.
- Get professional help.
- Change my phone number.
- Move.

4. Set due dates for each item on your list.

Everyone's situation is different, so you must be as aggressive as necessary to make the needed changes in your life in good time. I know a man facing his third felony. If convicted, he could serve up to life in prison. He is now on probation, and if he gets caught using drugs or alcohol or getting into any other trouble while on probation prior to his court hearing, he will get hammered by the court. If I were in his shoes, I would do whatever it takes, today, right now, to get away from the source of my trouble.

- Stay away from people who drag me down.
  - Due by: Today
- Stay away from the partyers in my life.
  - Due by: Today
- Start going to a Christian church.
  - Due by: This weekend
- Read every scripture in the Bible that speaks about drugs and alcohol.
  - Due by: 3/15/10
- Join a Christian support group like Celebrate Recovery.
  - Due by: 3/30/10
- Find Christian friends to hang out with.
  - Due by: 4/15/10
- Find a sponsor or accountability partner.
  - Due by: 3/15/10
- Get professional help if need be.
  - Due by: 4/30/10
- Change my phone number.
  - Due by: 3/15/10
- Move.
  - Due by: 5/30/10

5. For each item, write out how you think you can accomplish it.

This is the "action" part of your Action Plan. For example, Number 1 on this list is "Stay away from people who drag me down." I had to move and change my phone number to get away from the crazy partyers in my life. What will it take for you?

As you write out your Action Plan, do it in simple terms. Again, this is for you to accomplish your goal, not to impress others. Now, meet with someone you trust and go over it with him or her. Ask for their improvement suggestions. Take any suggestions to heart, and revise accordingly.

OK, now you have a plan. If your accountability partner is the person you reviewed your Action Plan with, then great! You are ready to get going. If not, find someone to fill this role and get started.

You can use this format for simple or complex goals. Your Action Plan can be as simple as the one below and still have a life-changing effect.

ACTION PLAN

Goal: Make new Christian friends who don't drink or take drugs or break the law just for fun.

Steps to Accomplish Goal:

Step 1.   I will commit to finding new Christian friends who will encourage me in the right direction.

When: I will start this weekend, 3/29/2010.

How: By going to church instead of out to party.

Step 2.   I will find a church that is Bible-based, has a great worship service at least once a week, and that I feel comfortable with.

When: I will start this weekend, 3/29/2010.

How: I will go every Sunday and Wednesday night if they meet midweek until I find the church for me. Then I will be a regular member and stick to it.

Step 3.   I will attend all the church functions. It may be difficult at first, but I will do it.

When: I will start this weekend, 3/29/2010.

How: I will get a schedule of all the church functions and go to all of them that apply to me.